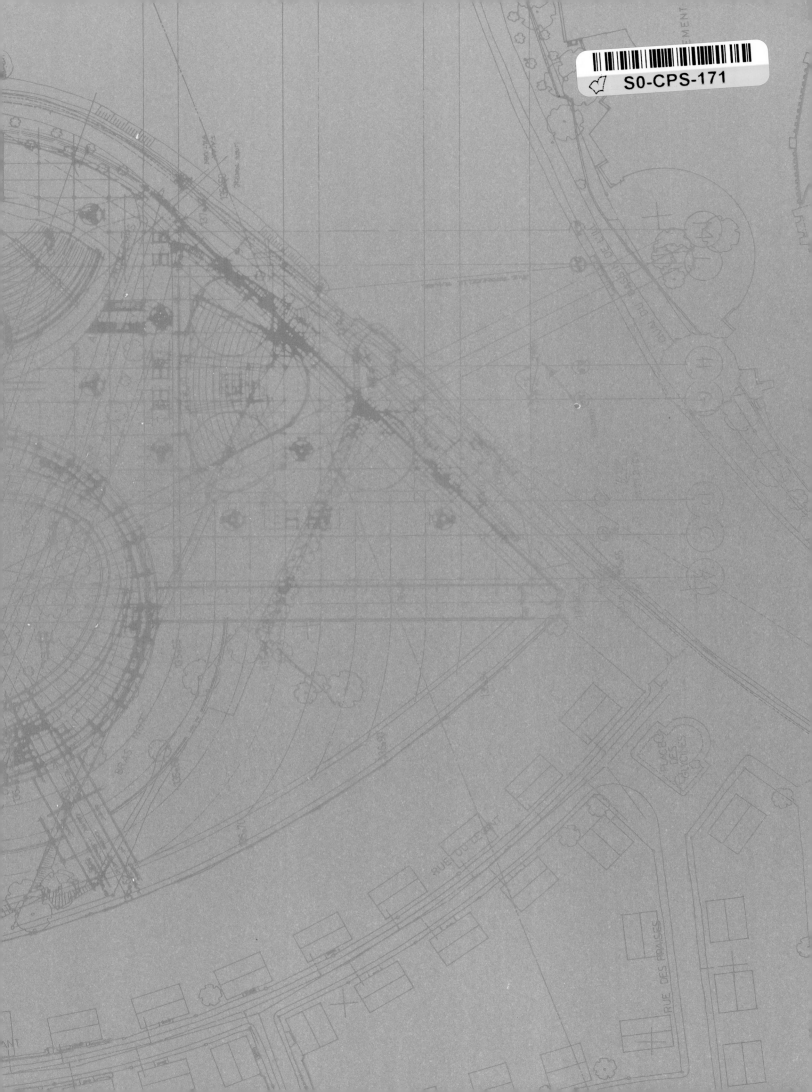

ARCHITECTURE • STUDIO

Selected and Current Works

ARCHITECTURE STUDIO

Selected and Current Works

Introductions by Masayuki Fuchigami and Mario Pisani

First published in Australia in 1996 by
The Images Publishing Group Pty Ltd
ACN 059 734 431
6 Bastow Place, Mulgrave, Victoria, 3170
Telephone (61 3) 9561 5544 Facsimile (61 3) 9561 4860

National Library of Australia Cataloguing-in-Publication Data

Architecture Studio.
    Architecture Studio: Selected and current works.

    Bibliography.
    Includes Index.
    ISBN 1 875498 39 7
    Master Architect Series II ISSN 1320 7253
    720.92

Edited by Patricia Sellar
English translation by Lucien Collard
Japanese translation by Yukie Chapman, Kei Knight
InLingua Text
Iconography (Paris): Carol Guinebert, Stéphane Zamfirescu

Designed by Laurent Marrier d'Unienville for Blur Pty Ltd,
with The Graphic Image Studio Pty Ltd,
Mulgrave, Australia
Film separations and printing by Everbest Printing H.K.

Contents

Contents

Firm Profile

INTRODUCTION

Interview with Architecture Studio

By Masayuki Fuchigami

M asayuki Fuchigami, an architect and architecture critic established in Tokyo, has travelled all over the world and is acquainted with many architectures. He has written mainly on contemporary architects and architecture. He is the chief editor of *Compe & Contest*, a review devoted to architectural competitions, the only one of its type in Japan.

Masayuki Fuchigami

A few years ago, in a review of French architecture, I discovered a very futuristic and ultramodern architecture—the High School of the Future. It looked like a Concorde. I was very surprised by the shape of that project. We Japanese have difficulty in conceiving such bold shapes for the design of a school. It was the High School of the Future that first made me want to get to know Architecture Studio.

Masayuki Fuchigami

I would like to know your general perception of architecture.

Architecture Studio

Architecture today is first of all a social thing that results as much from a conflictive process as from the expression of a consensus.

Conflicts are inevitable and necessary: the dynamic that springs from the contradictory dialogue of economic, cultural and social interests fits in with the project, imparts information to it and precludes its autonomy.

But the production of space through the consensus that it establishes presupposes a will that transcends individuals. It bears testimony, at a given moment, to a shared cultural reality. This is what gives it its specificity, not a supposedly 'artistic' manipulation of shapes.

We are stimulated by the collective dimension of the job and by working on sites that have a collective dimension.

Vis-a-vis the aesthetic dimension, we affirm the primacy of the cultural dimension in architecture.

The education and regulation of beauty no longer exist.

We do not believe that it is possible to create one or several codes of aesthetics, we believe in a transfer of values across present-day creative disciplines, we believe in intercultural correspondences, we believe in the poetry of a situational architecture.

We are not in favour of a single idea or a single model, whether it be political or formal.

Our leanings indicate the uncertainty of (philosophical, formal) plurals and denote both simplicity and diversity.

Our discourse is centred on what underlies our actions that are themselves uncertain, conflictual, complex.

We like theories but fight against doctrine and dogma.

The following are a few fragments of our thinking, a few keys to our architecture:

Concept

A means of repelling intuition as much as possible (see *Method*).

After the inevitable constraints of a programme have been stated, the concept is the idea of the project, what matters above all, what gives rise to the project even before it has been designed. This preliminary conceptualisation of the project is made indispensable by the group's design method.

Artists

We do not profess to be artists, we are architects. It is a profession.

The field of architecture must be opened up.

Architecture is made with the city, the landscape, the colours, the furniture, the design, the techniques...

Possibilities

No data on a context or way of thinking, even if it appears to be negative, should be rejected out of hand. We endeavour, through our work, to reveal all the potentialities afforded by a problematic.

Contradictions

Ambiguities resulting from the dual interpretation of a building, its obvious signs and its deep nature, its autonomy and its contextualism. If there is often a dissonance between the facade and the interior, or even along the same path, if there is nearly always a lack of identity—or indeed a deliberate confusion— between the expression of constructive functions and those that are characteristic of the plastics of the materials, we think it is because a building should not be read like a machine, a scale model, a drawing, the demonstration of a single theory. We think that it is perceived in its different scales, from a number of distances and proximities, and that the 'codes' are not the same. We place it in a close, but often disturbing, relationship with the context. The relationship depends on the topology, the town planning—we accept, for example, that a new building is affected by the layout, size and other constraints of a site. We highlight these things. The disturbance could be caused by a sudden change in style, the choice of techniques and the expressiveness of materials and also by the partitioning of rhythms and the introduction of a narrative that does not suit the history of the site and belongs by rights to the building.

Method

Our will to practise a collective mode of architectural design requires the use of a method, the necessary tool for group work, a language base that permits all of us to understand each other and to progress in successive layers.

'Red-lining'

A kind of x-ray of the project, a preliminary regulating outline enabling the control and co-ordination of all the sitings of the various elements of the project, both sectionally and longitudinally (structures, layout, partitions, ducts, doors, stairs, lift...), the outcome of the initial design phase, this document—which is regularly updated—serves as a basis for all project drawings.

Autonomy

We are completely opposed to buildings designed as a whole, and built anywhere, totally unconnected to anything.

Harmony

The search for harmony may be dissonant. The raison d'être of harmony is not the 'enjoyment' of shapes and volumes. It is also an attempt to meet a social demand—whether expressed or not.

It is a negotiation between the different parameters of the context of a project.

'Good taste'

An eternal debate, a label to avoid, conformist versus traditional. Always remember this quotation from Victor Hugo, which borders on provocation: "Ugliness is beauty".

Tabula rasa

To the yawning gap of the *tabula rasa* approach, we always prefer the complexity (interrogation, uncertainty) of the city and the uncontrolled confrontations of the suburbs, the accumulation of memory values, the stratification of meaning.

Limits

Limits interest us. Going all the way—good taste, technology..., to the verge of imbalance.

Masayuki Fuchigami

What are your inspirations or the creative origins that influence you the most?

Architecture Studio

Generally speaking, we are influenced by culture, or cultures, and we continue to draw from these sources without there being a need to define a single origin, or to limit them in time or duration.

For us, architecture has broken its isolation to open up to other artistic and intellectual fields. The approaches of artists like James Turrell or Robert Irwin, for example, seem very close to our own preoccupations, as are some analyses by Michel Serres and by René Girard.

We are influenced by the production of our contemporary society, whether it be through architectural and urban phenomena or through theatrical, economic, social, etc. creations.

Moreover, these influences can vary from one project to the next and our group benefits from contributions by each of the personalities that make it up.

But the basis of our approach and the inspiration for each project also depend greatly on the ambient context. We are referring to the economic, social, cultural context, the client or contracting authority and the specific challenges of the operation, as well as the site topography, its orientation and physical environment.

We claim that for each project we create something truly unique because of the complex relationship and the synthesis that we institute between all the elements of its genesis.

Thus a superficial reading of our architecture in purely formal terms is meaningless if the other 'dimensions' of the project are not taken into account.

The critical role of architecture and its significant dimension are fundamental even if we also recognise the intrinsic value and manner of art.

Masayuki Fuchigami

Among world architects—dead or alive—who influenced you the most and how?

Architecture Studio

In the light of what we have just said, our answer might be "all" or "no one in particular". It is an operative question and not a matter of principle or sentiment, although everybody has his or her preferences. We are not really interested in architects as such, we are interested in architectures. All architectures, no matter how big they may be, are not equally relevant under the same conditions of construction and scheduling.

In other words, for us, the future of architecture is not in architecture.

Masayuki Fuchigami

What do you think of Japanese culture or the differences between France and Japan?

Architecture Studio

We are fascinated by Japanese culture. It seems to be continually developing, precariously balanced on a razor's edge, oscillating between tradition and modernism (and for us Westerners, this modernism has certain futuristic characteristics that it owes to its very extremism), spirituality and consumer society, nature and megalopolises, etc....

Japan is a country where extremes meet. As architects and town planners, we are sensitive to the spatial and urban implications of these power relationships.

Japan's large cities, one could say the conurbation along the Pacific coast, provide an example of uncontrolled town planning which is completely inconceivable in the West but salutary— inasmuch as it is topical and contemporary—for us who live in Baron Haussmann's seemingly well laid-out Paris. It expresses what our culture has a tendency to play down, all the violence and barbarity generated by infrastructures and speculation.

At the same time, Japan would not survive if these built-up areas were not structured by something else. Augustin Berque wrote that "Japanese cities express nature", which sounds paradoxical but expresses an 'inner' reality.

Whilst the Japanese have assimilated the achievements of Western architecture, notably through the modernist movement, it seems to us that the reverse path would be enriching.

All these cultural differences fuel our curiosity and stimulate our architectural appetite. We would very much like to build in Japan. In our eyes, it would mean a new freedom in certain respects, far from the constraints of the 'museum city' for example, and the need for a thorough cultural rethinking because of this East/West interface.

Architecture Studio

By Mario Pisani

Architecture Studio is currently experiencing particularly intense and happy times. The members who make up the agency are the material expression of a radical change that has taken place, over the last few years, in architecture in France, where not only the clients and contracting authorities but also the public are involved in initiatives that are talked about and that strike the collective imagination.

Included among the representatives of this change are Jean Nouvel—with whom Architecture Studio built the Institute of the Arab World in Paris (1981–1987)—and Christian de Portzamparc, the creator of The City of Music, who received the prestigious Pritzker award for his works that are deeply rooted in French culture.

All contributed new ideas that made architecture evolve. They changed the expression of taste and took a critical look at architecture.

What differentiates them from the former is the attention they devote to sites, a rich source of inspiration, and their desire to build urban dramas and episodes and not just plain architectural objects, even if they were perfect. They have understood that they need to think in terms of urban landscapes—so much more complex and attractive.

The technological soul to bring science closer to man, a 'soft' technology, a boundless passion for the present which has lost none of its attractiveness but fulfils an interest in history, brings them closer to the latter.

These architects illustrate one possible path, situated somewhere between continuity and renewal.

Their agency is located in the Rue Lacuée, not far from the Place de la Bastille, in a magnificent setting—a former hothouse for oriental plants turned into a locksmithing business and featuring a central space, a succession of galleries, all teeming with life.

Architecture Studio is comprised of Martin Robain, Rodo Tisnado, Jean-Francois Bonne, all three nearly fifty, who have belonged to the group since its inception in 1973. They were recently joined by Alain Bretagnolle, René-Henri Arnaud and Laurent-Marc Fischer, all about thirty and brimming with talent.

At present, having won the international competition for the European Parliament in Strasbourg, Architecture Studio is supervising the construction operations, a work that will mark the future of architecture with the force of its overall image and its technological innovations. An element of great density in the agency's conceptual experience, the Parliament creates a 'before' and an 'after' its existence, and symbolises a 'rite of passage'.

Mention must also be made of their entry in the competition for the construction of new churches on the outskirts of Rome.

It is now several months since the Jules Verne High School at Cergy-le-Haut has been completed, where the name of the famous writer has become a source of inspiration for a large-scale architectural story that is in symbiosis with the great author's writings.

In Paris, a bilingual active school and 79 apartments, in the 15th arrondissement, are starting to be inhabited by 'warm' human lives, an example of a world rich in potential dialogue, while a post office and mail sorting centre are already operating at full capacity, a very interesting building that stands out because of its refusal to make concessions to form.

A hive of activity, the Gennevilliers fire station is a condenser, an urban signal, an efficient agglomerate in an area without clear-cut borders, that abandoned its rural origin to turn into something else.

One begins to wonder, when one sees the quality and quantity of their production, if one of the reasons for the pregnancy of this architecture is not the methodology used, the work in common that brings together the most diverse experiences. Architecture Studio has remained a collective structure that favours dialogue and confrontation of the individuality of its members.

This approach obviously has many advantages.

For the strength of the group is that reasoning is developed, amplified and enriched. The final solutions that are adopted are never those of a single individual but have been weighed up by several people, each of whom has made his own contribution. This internal criticism is very productive as each idea is thrown at the group; the result is a complete freedom that nevertheless meets the collective requirement.

Thanks to the methodology used, ideas progressively become clearer and are selected; the best, the strongest ideas, those that can resist the sting of criticism finally prevail. The final outcome is born of this confrontation: intense, continually renewed and different from one project to the next.

This method and the group work undeniably bear the mark of the enthusiasm of 1968, when it was believed, amidst the total confusion, that change was at hand.

This is when our friends met in architecture faculties; they discussed not only fundamental questions, the great ideal options, but also everyday life, the possibility of freeing oneself, of throwing off the constraints that characterise industrial societies, such as repetition which brings about alienation, dependence when making choices, hierarchy in functions—architecture is not immune to any of this.

Ten years later, in France as in Europe, ideas and consciences were conditioned by the backwash, the disappointed hopes. The *tabula rasa* was supplanted by individualism, cynicism, etc. While in the 1930s the team concept—an idea dear to William Morris—had gained acceptance as an essential component of modern projects, one wonders why architecture ended up creating a kind of 'star system', as in the cinema, fashion, the record industry, which tends to promote just the person, in the fine arts spirit against which we had fought so hard in 1968.

We are convinced that it is not by chance that the European Parliament, the strongest symbol of this strange community of peoples, often fighting each other and at least continually arguing, will be built by representatives from a civilisation that is the bearer of all other ideas.

The European Parliament in Strasbourg is a moment of great strength for Architecture Studio. This building complex explores the perimeters, the uncertain borders of two archetypes: the tower and the pyramid which will metamorphose into a cylinder surrounding an elliptical square and an incline covering the hemicycle.

These volumes are often used in designing highly representative edifices, for, in addition to their monumental aspect, they identify essential cosmic symbols.

The Parliament project took those figures as a starting point and developed them by transforming those archetypes that talk about mediation between life and death, between rationality, which calls up geometry as a method of constructing science, and fancy, which permits the unbridled invention of images, between rules and exceptions to rules, all of which provide the impetus for the development of architecture. This project which, because of its complexity, could not be the agency's first assignment, occupies a central position. Let us take the story from the beginning.

When Architecture Studio won the competition for the Parliament in 1991, it had already built the nursery and primary school in Paris (1982–1985) where the orthogonal layout grid appeared, at once affirmed and denied. It conjures up the matrices of Rationalism, which allude to the possibility of perceiving the universe through a structure that enables objects to resume their own characteristics, those of their usage value, not their exchange value. But here the grid is lightened by colour which distinguishes it from, and opposes it to, the typical whiteness of rationalistic architectures. This linguistic element is further unbalanced by a freehand 'promenade' that breaks the rigidity, the schematism of the plan; finally, upside-down Doric capitals of some kind, placed at the foot of external pillars, add a touch of irony to the whole. The grid is also one of the salient features of the "Tête de la Défense" project (1983). The grid, in its slow ascent to the sky, tends to lose its consistency, to become immaterial. It can then be regarded as an extraordinary poetic expression, an allusion to Lyotard's theories on total languages that are put in a difficult situation by the arrival of minor languages.

In the Institute of the Arab World, which has an extraordinary relationship with its context, the grid becomes a kind of filter that operates like a sunbreaker in the inner courtyard and has marble slabs attached to it. The grid also plays a role in a game of union with the graphic elements of the Arab culture, which, through the use of photosensitive diaphragms, conjures up a *moucharabieh*.

Next the agency built the apartment building in the Rue du Château-des-Rentiers in Paris (1984–1985) where the exploration of the orthogonal layout grid continues in the form of a steel structure that climbs beyond the building—an element which is also present in the Parliament. At the High School of the Future, in the Parc du Futuroscope at Poitiers-Jaunay-Clan (1986–1987), the logic of the slightly inclined roof is one of the major components. The Arènes High School in Toulouse (1989–1991) is shaped like an ancient amphitheatre. In the latter projects, the search for forms already heralds the European Parliament. They are the natural antecedents of concepts that they already partly foreshadow and that will only need to be developed to arrive at the key ideas of this large undertaking. The Parliament is the result of a series of sedimentation processes and constitutes a veritable rite of passage, similar to that described by Conrad in *The Shadow Line* or those alluded to by Benjamin in his most emblematic work.

The reason for the density of the concept derives from the methodology used to represent the image of Europe—from the initial approach to more complex themes. There is an awareness that Western culture, which was born here, is certainly not the only one; it is, therefore, possible to represent one's contribution to universal history by the concept of Classicism, beginning with the Greek ideal of *kalos kagathos*, the indissoluble link between ethical and aesthetical values, and by the concept of Baroque, interpreted as dream, whim, fancy.

Architecture Studio goes back in time to find the most significant moments of European culture, when Classicism and Baroque met and became integrated. Maybe our architects had in mind Scott's definition in his *Architecture of Humanism*: "The Renaissance eventually combined the picturesque with classical architecture itself and both blended to form the Baroque". By its tower, the European Parliament clearly evokes order, centrality, the very concept of power, but inside we find the ellipse—a reference to Kepler and the orbits of the planets but also a typical element of Baroque; the combination of the two elements results in Europe's most important contribution to world culture. In addition to the classical and baroque inspiration, the European Parliament also contains other important elements: the team's cultural knowledge is expressed in their relationship with the city, the suggestions of light, the interest for technology, the desire to tell a story. Finally, the Parliament contains the very concept of modernity, the idea of an open work, perfected by Umberto Eco, illustrated here by the cylinder and its layout, unfinished like Europe itself.

We refer here to something much more complex than a mere building. It is a real piece of city, for which urban characteristics must be taken into account; it is crossed by streets, numerous car parks are required, the technical networks must operate in an emergency situation. The building cannot be modified ad infinitum. It cannot be extended at will. It has its own morphological laws. The city must also be integrated into the building in order to go beyond architecture and to reason in terms of urban landscape. Other projects also draw their inspiration from this process, for example, the "La City" business centre in Besancon (1988–2000) which is a real quarter, a piece of city that comprises a bank, offices, a university, a residential estate and a hotel, always with a special concern for user-friendliness. The response of our architects is peculiar to the Architecture Studio culture, beginning with the emotion engendered by a work like Beaubourg, by the architectures of Stirling, Ando and Foster. They still believe, with the bulimia that characterises their work, that anything is possible.

One of the most emblematic elements of the current architectonic culture resides in the value attributed to the environment, as a reaction against the proliferation of soulless suburbs, large urban areas around towns designed as small centres and sometimes even in natural landscapes, and of a building style that trivialises localities, geographic areas and even the institutions and everyday living spaces. We could ponder the why and wherefore of this 'collapse of places', beginning with a false idea of the modernist culture and a project philosophy more concerned about the design of the architectural object than the effects of the work in its context.

By contrast, Architecture Studio has developed an interesting methodology by its way of posing problems, observing places in all their stratifications and the most varied elements that make up an environment—a true philosophy for starting a new project.

Our architects no doubt cite other factors such as the humours, the sensations, the ideas that create an atmosphere like the one we find at the Institute of the Arab World, a structure deeply rooted in its context, which can be approached in several different ways. First, a kind of formal homage to the Paris Faculty of Economics. Then a clever use of the available space to create a square that opens onto the Boulevard Saint-Germain. Finally, the curve of the facade —in the body of the building that houses the museum—follows the contours of the slow-moving Seine. In the disused and neglected harbour of Dunkirk, Architecture Studio designed the Citadel

University (1987–1990), on the mole, on Citadel Island. It was recently expanded (in 1994) according to the principles that made it successful. The starting point was, as always, the taking into account of the context where the big grey–blue expanse mingles with man's work. They were aware that the city is uniform only on the surface and it is impossible not to take the presence of water into consideration. Water that rumbles and resonates in the ironic fountain invented for the apartment building in the Rue du Château-des-Rentiers in Paris; water dreamed of, wished for, conjured up in the French Embassy in Muscat, in the Sultanate of Oman (1986–1989), a refreshing rivulet in the faljah which, in the Citadel University, is transformed into a giant wave of metal that does not conjure up shipwrecks but covers the building with a kind of protective blanket, the intensity of which changes according to the variations in the sky reflected in it. Here the site abandons the memory of a past that is not forgotten. Here we have a former tobacco warehouse that establishes a kind of continuity: the fathers who worked here hand over to their sons who study here. The ingenuity of Architecture Studio has transformed the site into a magical, enchanted place.

It is possible to find other concepts such as juxtaposition, superposition, inclusion which seem to re-enact the passage of time, the orchestra which through its instruments encompasses changes and conflicts. The musical score precludes neither dissonances nor breaks in rhythm and shows the image of a particularly fascinating evolutionary path made up of successive strata, like those in some early Christian cathedrals that were built on the foundations of pagan temples, then became Romanesque churches and finally came under the yoke of the Gothic style. That architecture thrives on spoliation and change, it phagocytises and digests what it has found in situ and regurgitates it in different forms.

Again it is memory—the image of the bullfighting amphitheatre—remembrance as a light but effective way of keeping alive the traces of the past, that appears in the Communications High School or Lycée des Arènes in Toulouse. In a peripheral, discontinuous context, where buildings designed as 'plane-tables' have been placed on the site, with a single principle to govern their siting: the heliothermal axis, according to the precepts of modern town-planning. The remembrance of the ancient amphitheatre of Golden Sun that stood there and described a perfect circle, is evoked with sensitivity and finesse. The architects went back to those forms and proposed to integrate part of the ancient 'cavea' into the project, but shortly before work started, the ancient structure collapsed, so that the communications pole will soon cover the whole development land.

To the north of Paris, near the Porte de Clignancourt, along the ring road, Architecture Studio is studying a project for a university residence. The main principles: "Frame what you want to see, protect yourself against what you don't want to suffer". Again it is the site that determines the laws of architectural composition with a shield facing the ring road traffic, while three 11-storey buildings, beautifully streamlined, rise above a quiet, peaceful, green area.

The shield represents a kind of wall, a large-sized curved screen, designed to be seen briefly by motorists travelling on the ring road. Obviously, a refusal can transform itself into an architectural gesture, as obelisks did in times past and billboards more recently. Today, a large screen ready to disseminate its messages will be the landmark of the site. It will stand out not only because of its size (100 metres long by 30 metres high) but also by its ability to imprint itself on the collective imagination, as a new signal: the vicinity of the Porte de Clignancourt.

Ever since man invented the menhir or the cardo and the decumanus, light has been one of the raisons d'être of architecture.

Light plays an essential role in the works of Architecture Studio, so much so that we are justified in including it as one of the most important elements in their architectural compositions, starting for example with the solar house project (1980) or the palace of Prince Naif in Jeddah (1982) and the "Tête de la Défense" in Paris. Light is also fundamental in the Our Lady of the Ark of the Covenant Church in Paris (1986–1996), where one senses affinities with the sophisticated architecture of Tadao Ando, and also in the Saint George Seminary Church in Frankfurt am Main (1989) where we find a learned combination between the zenithal light and the light that filters through the stained glass windows, which echo the words of St John: "Jesus is the light of the world".

Is it possible to say something about the Institute of the Arab World that hasn't been said before? That each part is shaped by light: light emphasises the curvature of the arc-shaped facade, enhances our perception, helping us to understand what is meant by dynamic architecture; the break between the two wings of the building in the shade like a lane in the kasbah; the protected courtyard—a magical space—where a filtered light creates all around an intimacy seldom found in modern buildings; and, above all, the library facade with all its moving diaphragms.

To build this masterpiece, it may have been necessary to consult the light tables, that enabled Bernin—the undisputed master of this subject—to check his calculations. History has it that he lost them in Paris, at the time of his unsuccessful bid for the Louvre project, and that they were miraculously found in a second-hand bookshop by Le Corbusier who used them for the Ronchamp Chapel.

At the High School of the Future, the hours of the day are regulated by light. The architects have designed a kind of flying wing, an oval disc that slides on a travelling crane. Thus a segment of this large vessel is really able to move. The disc exposes the elliptical courtyard and measures the light inside according to the prevailing conditions. Then, at the end of its run, it creates a kind of protected area, sheltered from the sun on one of the platforms used by students during the lunch break and where they can have impromptu parties. It is difficult not to see in this kind of hymn to the sun, these eclipses, these daily appearances, a symbol of the season cycle and life itself.

The particularly intense light also plays an essential role in the French Embassy in Muscat. The vast building stands not far from the sea, at the edge of the desert and under a relentless sun the burning heat of which must be tempered. Architecture Studio invented a kind of slightly inclined carpet that unfolds all along the land. This flying carpet, made of reinforced concrete and supported by frail columns, houses the chancery offices and the ambassador's residence which is crowned by a dome. A light portico projects shadows that flutter about. The portico invites us to enter a space that continually plays on the contrast between light and shade, enriched by the presence of colours. The 'carpet' is full of holes like a *moucharabieh*, veiled by differently-coloured windows. The atmosphere thus created conjures up the magical setting of the *Thousand and One Nights*. The light and shade, the colours, the water of the fountain and the palm trees help to create an exotic 'urban' landscape that is, nevertheless, linked to Western culture in the correct proportions that appear to be a hallmark of the art of Architecture Studio.

The need to dim the light, to moderate its intensity according to requirements is an imperative also found at the Citadel University in Dunkirk. The building is arranged around two wide streets, intersecting at right angles, that serve the premises, the stairs and the lifts. Swamping the lot, the wave breaks on the old tobacco warehouse. Above the streets, the wave appears to ripple, move, vibrate. Thus a kind of venetian blind is formed which can be controlled mechanically to enable the light to penetrate inside. The combination of different sources of light in the same space follows the example of Bernini, as in the Cornaro Chapel where the play between direct and reflected light is a quest for the "own particular light" of things.

In recent times, architecture has retreated into silence, isolation, aphasia. When strolling through the city, we no longer experience the sensations felt by Aragon or Baudelaire, the eulogists of the modern-day metropolis. Buildings are apathetic, silent, devoid of meaning; they express only the absurdity and mercenary mentality of the obsessive, worn-out typologies that mould the urban fabric throughout the world. The language of the modern world is universal, unrelated to places, it continually repeats the same phrases, it has deprived buildings of their symbolic value, invalidated the framework of its meanings, and has put a stop to our very fondness for narration that appeared when the world was in its infancy, when architecture began, when man erected columns, invented an order. Architecture has been reduced to the most trivial expression of functional necessities, deprived of its role to express the spirit of the times and the intrinsically human values.

Today architecture is returning to the expression of meanings, reappropriates decoration, entertains a relationship with history, operates in harmony with the sites or even succeeds in creating them, has a balanced relationship with technology and, above all, it has started telling us stories again.

The apartment building in the Rue du Château-des-Rentiers in Paris tells us about the metropolis, the danger of getting lost in it as one might in an inextricable forest, as if it were a real-life experience. The Stimuli is reminiscent of those years, an investigation into the city, "a manifestation full of contradictions", searching for empty space, vacant blocks, unbuilt areas on which the adventure of the project can be told. The desire to tell a story turns into a large topographical map of the 13th arrondissement covering a whole facade where underground stations are indicated by red lights: "Tolbiac", "Place d'Italie", "Campo Formio". Obviously, this facade is not only a subject for poetic response but it also works together with the whole building like a large fresco that is meant to tell us a story.

The High School of the Future tells us about the emergence of the new and the marvellous that we encounter during a voyage into the night, into the land of dream and lethargy, which may not make us any happier but attenuates the daily humdrum. The quest for the new characterises the relationship of man with time, till the present, right up to the spectral images of *Blade Runner*, Ridley Scott's film revelation. The plane, a kind of spaceship parked in the Parc du Futuroscope, enables the protagonist to flee from this territory beyond the metropolis, with one of those provisional angels.

In the Citadel University in Dunkirk, in that old tobacco warehouse saved in order to preserve, in the emerging new structures, a sign of the past, a memory of the place, the space tells us about the myth of the labyrinth. In that volume of the mind, from which all partitions and floors have been removed, leaving only support structures, wooden posts and frail beams, one feels that here anything can happen, even—as has been the case—a return to life.

The European Parliament project which, as we stated earlier, is a piece of city more than just a building, tells us many fascinating stories. For example, in its relationship with water, it rediscovers the eternal myth of Narcissus and self-love, one of the most poignant myths of Greek civilisation, our mother and companion. The eternal relationship between love and death where the discovery of the body and its beauty carries with it that of the image: of the evanescence of the shadow silhouetted against the contours of being.

It also tells us about the place: after climbing the stairs of this large stylobate, after getting past the cylinder that surrounds it, creating a filter, there appears the large ellipse, reminiscent of the teeming Baroque, the meeting place, as Abruzzese would say, "where gazes are exchanged". Beside myths, there was something else the Greeks valued greatly: an empty, sunny, dusty space where they exchanged goods and talked: a market, a square. Here, the sun is filtered by that large grid which signifies, like the unfinished parts of mosques and synagogues, ancient Christian crypts, a kind of *memento mori*. Dust is replaced by a covering, a kind of carpet that expresses on the ground the dream of walking on water.

The square designed as the pulsating heart of the city, driving force and nerve centre of the urban fabric is starting to interest architects again, after being eliminated by the modern movement. It is a privileged place for meetings, discussions, exchanges and it is therefore essential to an institution like the Parliament, to express its public function. It would appear that the moment announced by Benjamin has finally arrived: "We must still wait for the future to process the images of which the past is a repository". As far as the Parliament square is concerned, the waiting is over.

This is the message that Architecture Studio's architecture is trying to convey. In the Jules Verne High School, as well as in the "La City" business centre, the École des Mines and the Jean Monnet University in Saint-Étienne, it is patently obvious that the future has already begun and that it is processing images bequeathed by the past.

The images are capable of transmitting, to quote Calvino, "the meaning of the present which is also made of the accumulation of the past and the intoxication of the void of the future, the simultaneous presence of irony and anguish, in short, the manner in which the pursuit of a structural project and the imponderability of poetry become something unique".

SELECTED AND CURRENT WORKS

Super Stadium for the 1998 World Soccer Cup

International competition 1994
Paris-Saint Denis
Interministerial Delegation to the 1998 World Soccer Cup

The purpose of the Super Stadium is to host the 1998 World Soccer Cup, the Olympic Games and other large-scale events. It has an undercover seating capacity of 80,000 people and places the public as close as possible to the action. It also aims to structure a new district in the Saint-Denis Plain. Its role in the city is central to the project. It is symbolised by the similarity between its layout and that of the city.

Like the Spanish town's 'Plaza de Toros' or English colonial towns' cricket fields, the arena that surrounds the game area initiates the urban contour. The rectangle of the lawn, the oval of the stands, and outside, two simple figures, the circle of the amphitheatre and the square of the roof structure the geometry of the city. The anamorphosis of the volumes defines complex spaces, rigorous purities of structure.

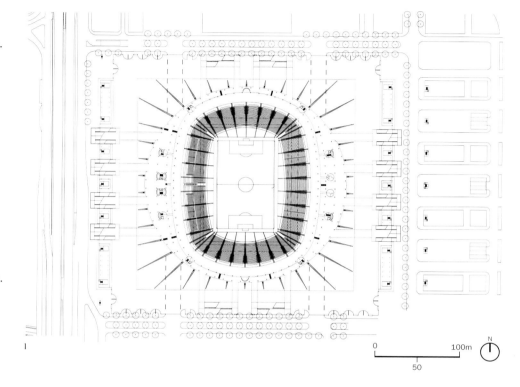

0   50   100m   N

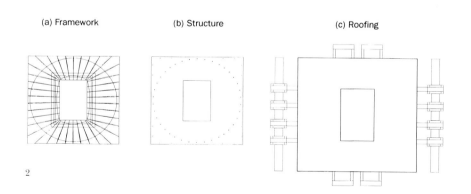

(a) Framework   (b) Structure   (c) Roofing

2

1   Plan of esplanade level
2   A simple figure: circle and square
3   General view
4   Aerial view of stadium and surroundings
5   View of entrance

3

4

5

The roof juts out from the area covered by the stadium to house four huge urban loggias in the same line as the concrete forecourt with overhangs of more than sixty meters. Its flat covering, accurately aligned in height with the rooftops of the Saint-Denis Basilica, represents a landmark in the plain, a white line above the horizon. The permeability and the intricacy of the spaces are reinforced by the wreath of lateral entry ramps and the associated buildings which form the real facade of the Super Stadium. The profile of the arenas is indented to the south and the north to place spectators in the city space, between the lights of Paris and those of Saint-Denis.

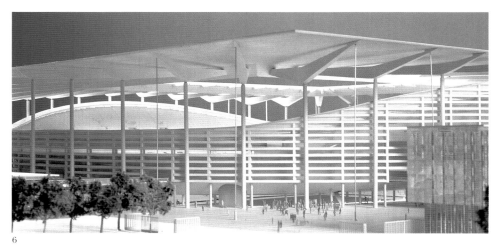
6

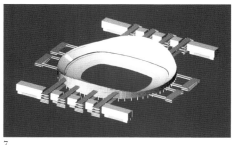
7

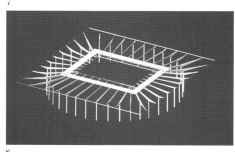
8

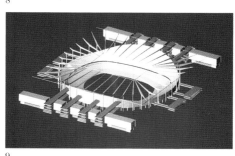
9

(a) Playing field

(b) Amphitheatre

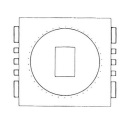
(c) Square

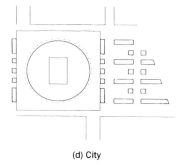
(d) City

10

11

12

Scenography for the "Press review: A report on information clearing-houses" exhibition

Design/Completion 1994/1994
Arsenal Pavilion, Paris
City of Paris, Arsenal Pavilion

The scenography for the "Press review" exhibition takes the visitor through and beyond the image, a media-staged ideal, to present and take apart media coverage strategies. It illustrates the exhibition's three leading themes on the architecture of the media: the public, the power, the production.

Entry is through a newspaper kiosk thereby immediately inviting you to visit the other side of the daily life. Visitors then discover the traffic lights of information as they watch an AFP videotex transmission in real time. Large stairs that step across a model of Paris lead directly to the first floor where the first space is a large parallelepiped with vertical walls forming a translucent composite material 'filter' that serves as a projection screen for the 'mediatisation' of the exhibition.

This space is dominated by a globe of the earth, symbol of worldwide information. This first environment defines a 'media sphere' in which all reality appears transposed.

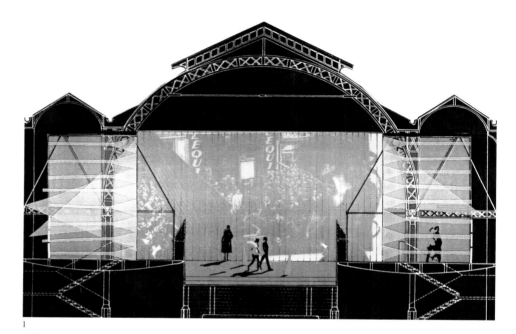

1

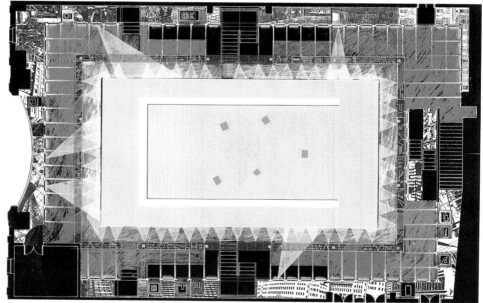

2

After crossing this virtual wall of an ideal world, one discovers the image transformation 'machinery', animated gridwork of machines used to capture, project, deviate, filter and transform images and reality which is representative of media techniques and creates a fun event through the diversity of the optical, mechanical, electronic elements brought into play, enabling visitors to grasp the different stages of the exhibition. This machinery is opened by gaps allowing visitors to reach the space of reality, that of the exhibition where they are shown documents and models, often original and never shown before, that present by theme the most remarkable buildings that house or have housed medias throughout the world.

3

4

5

6

1   Cross-section
2   First floor plan
3   Video and liquid crystal monitor in 'machine room'
4   Projection onto the 'filter'
5   'Media sphere' central space
6   Traffic between 'machine room' and 'filter'

Church

Design/Completion 1994/2000
Rome, Italy
Vicariate of Rome
1,500 square metres

This was one of the award-winning projects in the competition for the construction of 50 churches in Rome organised by the Vicariate of Rome. The project includes a church proper, complete with a multi-purpose hall, classrooms and the vicarage. It is located in one of the unfinished suburbs of the Italian capital. The church is part of this landscape, and is in the same line as the suburb's 'asphalt space'. It is a simple, cube-shaped, identifiable volume, surmounted by a spire. It is visibly a church in the city, asserting that role. The metal grid shell suggests the immateriality of the programme. The inside is in the archetypal tradition of Architecture Studio's church studies.

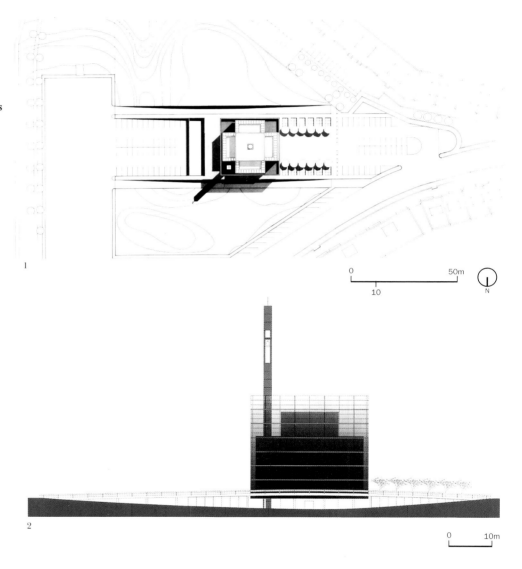

1   Block plan
2   Longitudinal section on ramp
3   Aerial view
4   Cross-section
5   View from the street

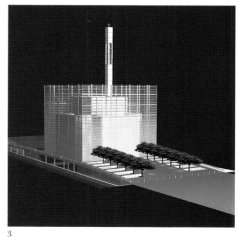

Its volume is a three-dimensional Greek cross, one of the branches of which is the choir, the others being the nave, tribunes, chapel, portal—which extends like a Latin cross into the parvis for open-air services. This uniting cross is defined by varied and independent space limits, thus conveying the church unity and its universal richness.

The treatment of light helps create this space where one is 'elsewhere' in the middle of the roman suburbs.

4

5

Rebuilding of souks

Design 1994
Beirut, Lebanon
Solidere
135,000 square metres

The project takes into account space and
time data, through the rebuilding of a place
—the souks—that still exists in the collective
memory. The magic of the souk roofs is
recreated by using a large 'plate' sloping
down towards the sea, accessible to the public,
a horizontal transposition of a *moucharabieh*
that supports the present-day upper town.
This 'plate' represents the upper town, the
reference for the stratification and unity of
the project. A free and autonomous space,
manifestly aligned with the scale of the city,
it gives the latter its urban character and
unity, while providing diversified activity
spaces. It is the roof of the souks, a magic
place, with a vista of the sea.

Endowed with a historical or archaeological
structure, the souk buildings are
rehabilitated, giving an architectural and
memorised character to the souks.
Synthesis of history and modernity, the
project bears in mind the context of the
city, all the while giving the communicable
vision of a contemporary Beirut.

1

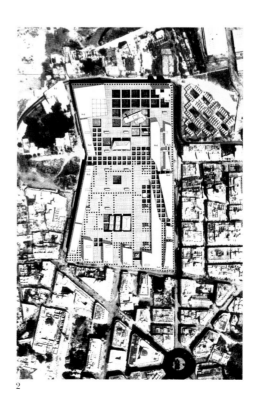

2

1   Ground floor plan
2   Block plan
3   Cross-section of lane in souk
4   Perspective view

3

4

Exhibition ground

Design 1993
Paris-Nord Villepinte
Paris-Nord Villepinte Exhibition Ground Operating Company,
Paris Chamber of Commerce and Industry
500,000 square metres

The very idea of staging a show or an exhibition is to present products, novelties, under the most attractive conditions. The notion of exhibition implies that of the future, of innovation.

The project expresses this relationship, new materials, new technologies; at the same time, it asserts its environmental mission, an exhibition-territory in a landscaped site.

Here, the place is an element of a communication system. The scale of the project demands the use of images, of photographic representation. The overall perception is virtual, media-inspired and expresses landscaping intentions. Particular, immediate perceptions are sensitive and assert the desire for a human, inviting architecture.

The exhibition ground offers a strong, efficient and exportable image that distinguishes it from a mere technological development.

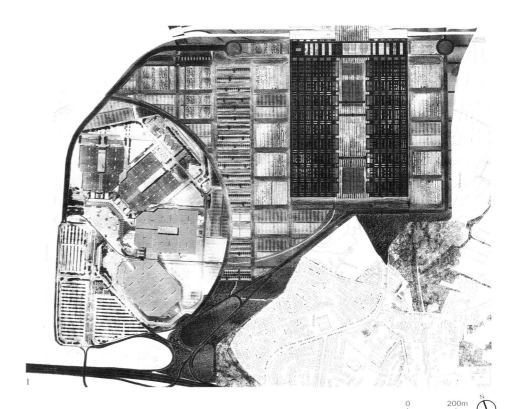

0   200m   N

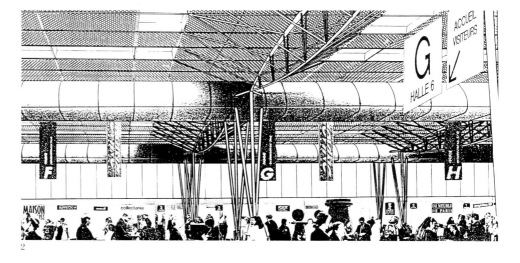

1   Block plan. Project 2
2   Exhibition hall perspective. Project 2
3   Overall plan. Project 2
4   Longitudinal sections and cross-sections. Project 2

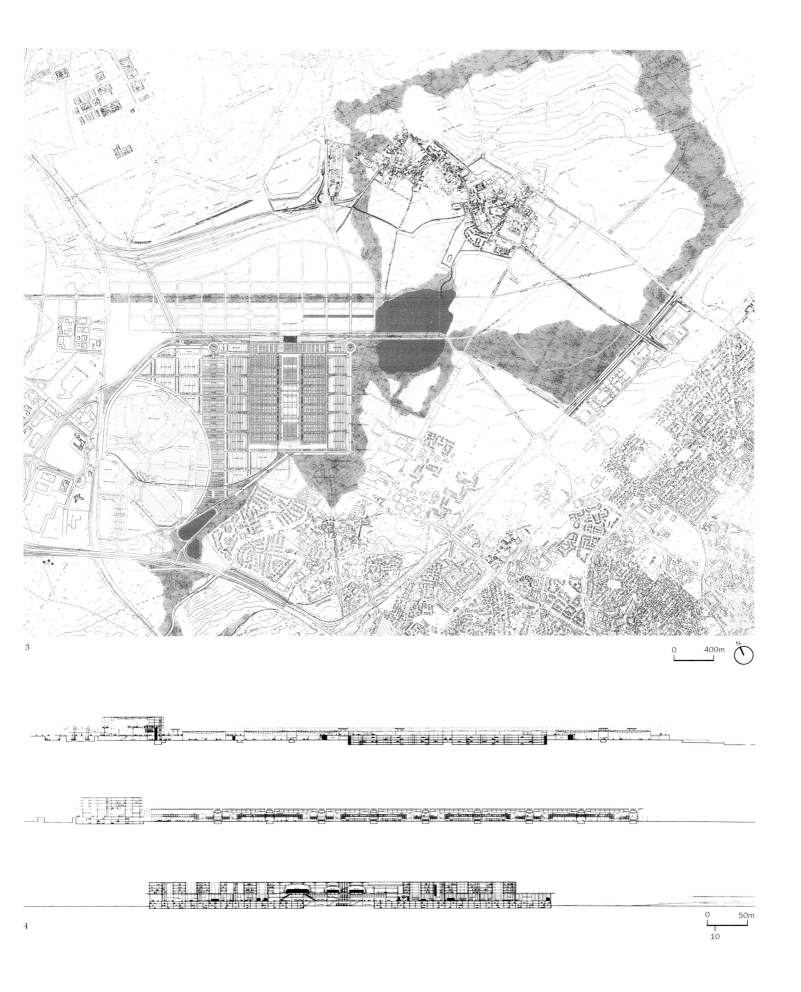

3

0   400m

N

4

0   50m

10

5

5 View of the hall. Project 1
6 View of the entrance. Project 1
7 Aerial view. Project 1

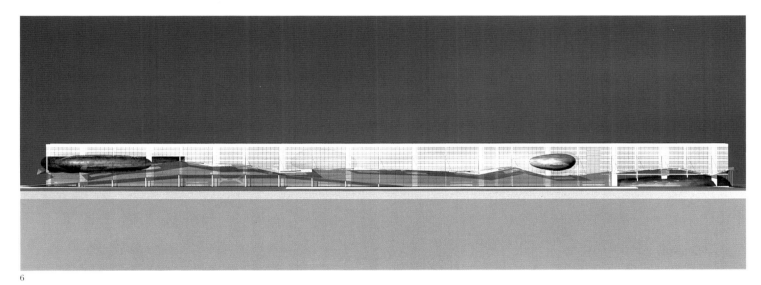
6

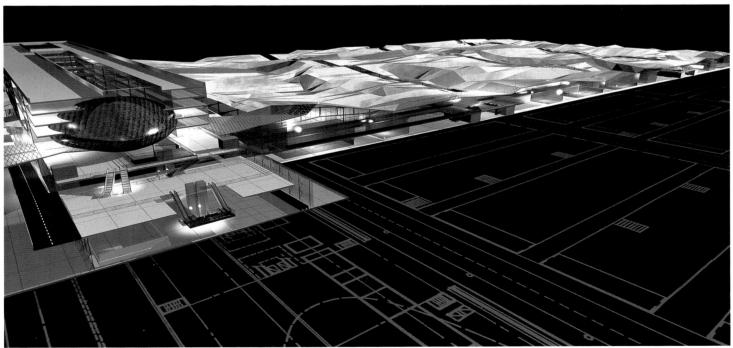
7

FIMAT office development

Design/Completion 1993/1994
Paris
FIMAT
600 square metres

The Hôtel de Bony, a Palladian mansion dating from the Restoration, is one of the remarkable products of the Parisian architecture of that period. Today it houses the FIMAT offices. They have been set up in a spirit of historical continuity that takes into account the main characteristics of the architecture, while adopting a contemporary development approach.

The original plan respects the axes of symmetry and the distribution according to Palladio's principles. The agency's contribution consisted of clarifying the original hotel plan by re-establishing the distribution of each level through a requalified central space: the anteroom.

1   R+2 level
2   R+3 level: roof space
3   Garden frontage

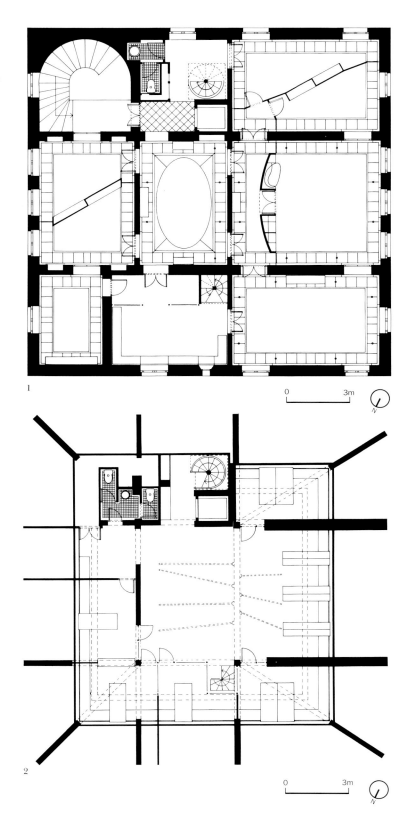

1

0   3m

2

0   3m

3

The Restoration decor has been reinterpreted by using its favourite materials, such as light-coloured wood marquetry, coloured glass, opalines, strong colours, and its decorative vocabulary and proportions—full and comfortable shapes.

These principles, attuned to the FIMAT Bank programme requirements, create spaces possessing a functional and hierarchical distribution and suitable for present-day use.

4

5

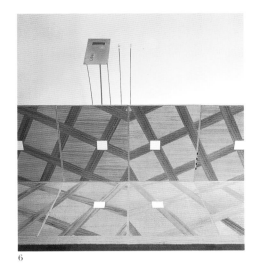

4 Anteroom
5 Serigraphed glass partition between central volume
  and offices
6 Air conditioning control, switch and technical
  skirting board
7 Great council room

6

7

Law Courts

Design/Completion 1993/1996
Caen
Ministry of Justice
9,500 square metres

A cornerstone of the Place Gambetta, the Law Courts (*Palais de Justice*) are a determining factor in the urbanisation of a new district.

The reflection on the monumentality of the judiciary institution, between autonomy and contextuality, gives rise to a strong, unifying image that is visible in varying degrees throughout the city.

The edifice is structured by three distinct orders that are superimposed and dialogue with each other.

The urban, contextual, order defines the external volumetry of the buildings in the area by means of horizontal rails that are the materialisation of the blueprint. The institutional order asserts the autonomy of the Law Courts in a particular and synthetic form emanating from its contextual frame. The internal order of the different jurisdictions is manifested on the outside in a cruciform geometry that distinguishes them and organises them into a hierarchy, thus signifying the content of the edifice.

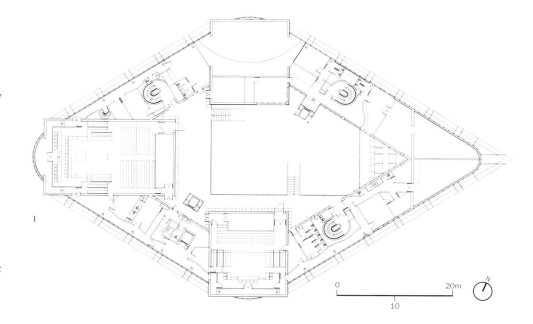

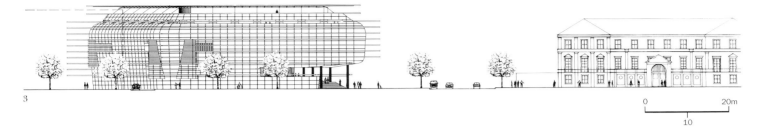

3

The Law Courts are arranged around a large atrium, a veritable urban piece situated in the same line as the square; the glass facades reflect the service activity of the institution. A walkway with a panoramic view of the city constitutes an open intermediary space. The architecture of the Law Courts gives to all the keys to its organisation and its specific function, thus breaking, through this rigorous 'structural transparence' of the various orders it is made up of, the image of an opaque, inward looking building.

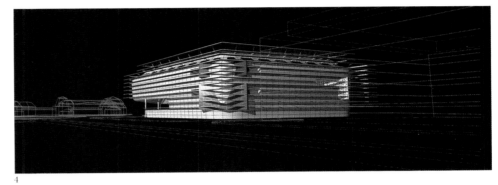

4

5

6

1   First level plan
2   Location plan
3   Eastern frontage
4   Perspective from the boulevard
5   View from the square
6   Internal view of atrium (study for the competition)

École des Mines

Design/Completion 1992/1995
Albi-Carmaux
Ministry of Industry and Foreign Trade
35,000 square metres

The École des Mines draws its inspiration from the rich local tradition while expressing in a strong and contemporary way the modernist values peculiar to Écoles des Mines.

The school mixes classical and modern references, a quest for balance between the timeless and the present, between history and modernity. This is an archetypal building that solves the faults that creates self-sufficiency from the city and self-sufficiency of each function. The school follows the logic and continuity of the city of Albi.

Its internal operation enables it to link the different functions without a break (brick spindle perpendicular to the covered street with the forum in the centre, in close contact with the external gallery: the warp).

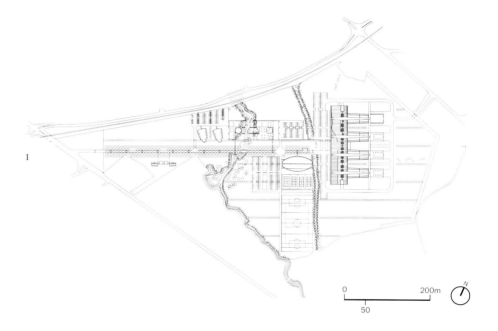

1   Block plan
2   Aerial view site (in December 1994)
3   R+1 level plan

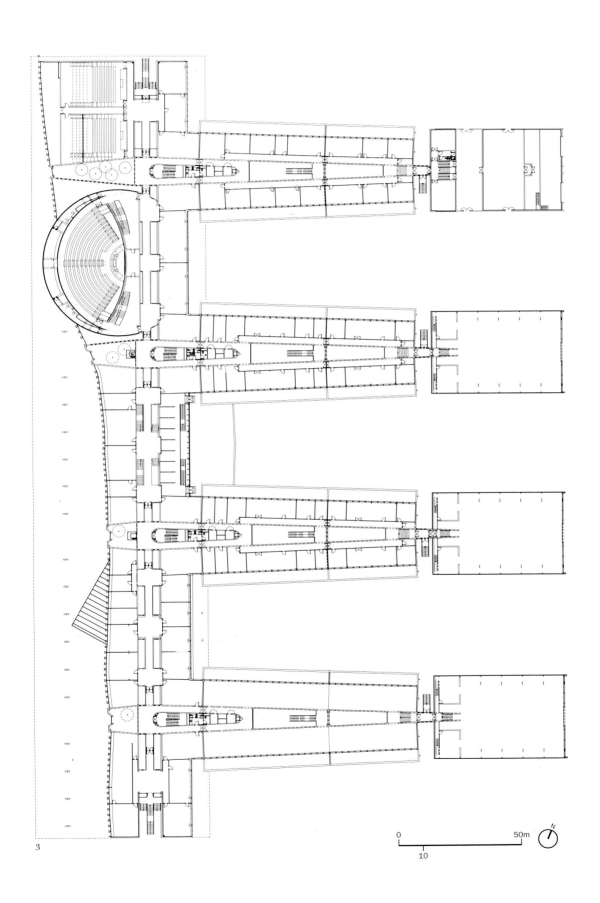

3

0   50m

10

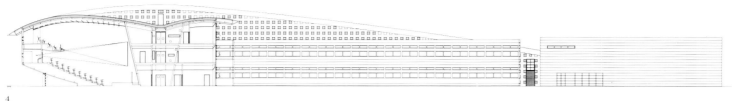

4

This duality between the cultures of the site—the thickness, massiveness of the city's brick walls, and the culture of the École des Mines, the transformation of matter, and development of new technologies —is the vehicle for a reflection and aesthetics that bring out significant, rich and stimulating oppositions, thus making it possible to define solutions that go beyond those stated by mere functionalism or regionalism.

5

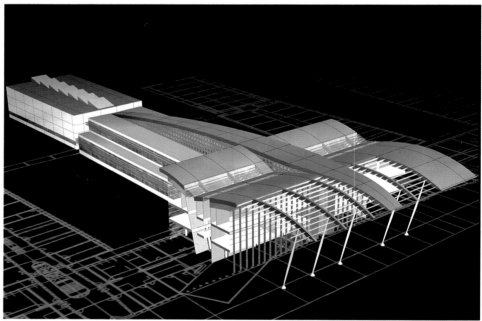

4   Lecture hall section
5   Aerial view
6   Axonometry
7   Eastern frontage
8   View of eastern frontage, by day
9   View of eastern frontage, by night

6

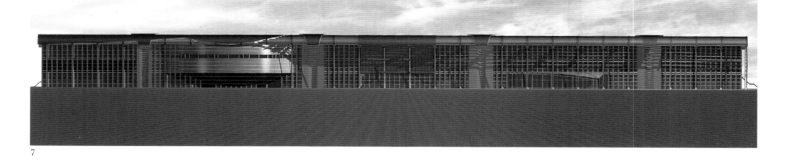

7

8

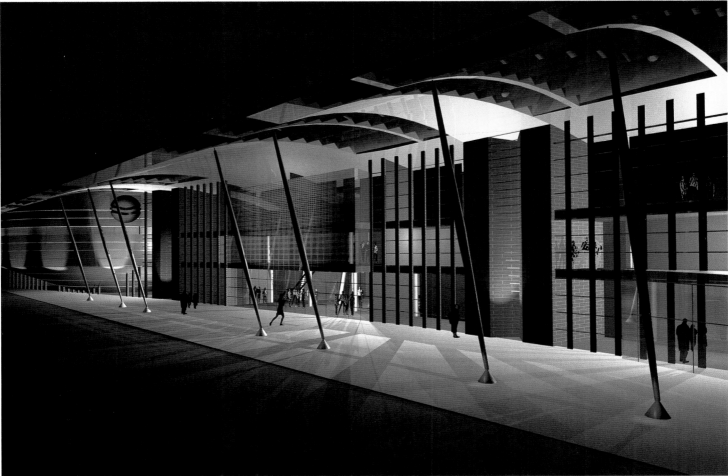

9

École des Mines   47

Libraries and completion
of Jussieu Campus project

Design 1992
Paris
Ministry of Culture and National Education
50,000 square metres

The location of the project, in the same line as the Institute of the Arab World, reinforces the theatrical nature of the university in the city. Facing the Seine, the library features a glass facade that is set at an angle to permit a better diffusion of daylight into the inner spaces. To assert the urban alignment of the Quai Saint-Bernard, a line of diodes that emit a blue light restores the virtual vertical of the building. A string of light crowns the facade and cycles through the names of great men, as well as announcing the cultural activities of the library.

Inside, the library offers a space bathed in light from a glass vault that soars towards the sky, a dynamic element signifying that knowledge is on the move. The light is diffused from the centre glass roof to all the reading rooms.

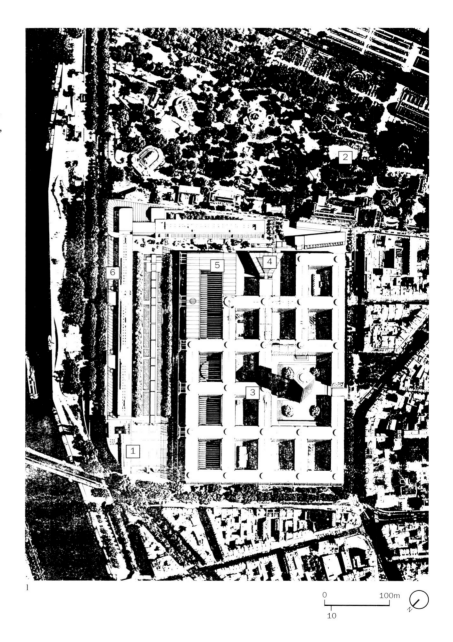

1

1 Institute of the Arab World
2 Plant garden
3 Existing campus
4–6 Projected library site

48

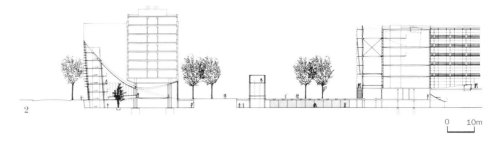

2

0   10m

3

The project is also intended to enrich the capital with a new urban green space on the same scale as Parisian gardens such as Palais-Royal, Place des Vosges or the Observatory: the Jussieu garden. The garden transposes the classical garden, its geometry asserting the linearity of space and the will of a transversal link.

It was important to rethink the facade of the University that gives onto the Seine and to create a new big garden on a site of rapture in Paris.

4

5

1   Block plan
2   Cross section of the north–south axis
3   Entrance foyer of building facing the river bank
4   Garden between faculty buildings
5   View from the Seine

Development of the Place de Francfort

Design 1992
Lyons
Rhône and Lyons District Road and Building Infrastructure Corporation
85,000 square metres

This project gave the opportunity to influence the town planning of the city of Lyons on different levels. It made it possible to complete the profile of the modern quarter of Part Dieu by means of slender twin towers and to treat the Place de Francfort as a true quality urban space. The two towers play both on the apparent similarity and the subtleties of the difference, on an impression of dynamism and the quest for serenity. The duality of these volumes is enriched by these significant oppositions and these contrasts, reflection and transparence, opaqueness and depth, linked and separated.

The monumentality is emphasised by the choice of simple, slender volumes that offer a peaceful and serene image of modernity.

The two towers are a landmark in the city of Lyons skyline, a monumental signal serving as a kinetic point of reference for the numerous lookouts in the area.

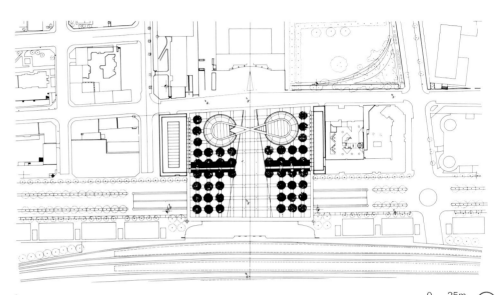

1

0   25m   N

2

1 Block plan
2 Perspective view of towers
3 View from the square
4–5 The two high rise blocks in the city skyline

4

5

3

City of Paris School of Fine Arts

Design 1992
Paris
City of Paris
18,000 square metres

The project is in keeping with a dialectic between history and the future of the city the symmetry of which is a major element. Before the building was burnt down, the two general stores represented an ideal counterpoint to the centrality of Ledoux's Rotunda situated at the other end of the basin. The project recreates this symmetry while preserving the mark of history. The school is housed in two identical and symmetrical contemporary buildings, located on either side of the Villette Basin, exactly where the former general stores stood.

As a counterpoint to this urban and historical continuity, the school is designed as a single entity where the two buildings are linked to one another by a high square that spans the canal. This square is a mobile deck the movement of which punctuates school life and makes it possible to preserve the urban perspective of the canal.

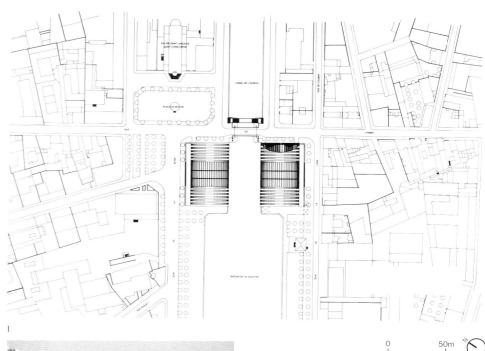

1

2

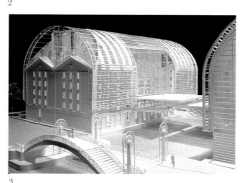

3

1   Block plan
2   View from Villette Basin
3   Footbridge between the two buildings
4   Facade of eastern building
5   The two buildings, with raised footbridge
6   View from Villette Basin

4

Movement, expression of modernity, is written here into the history and the environment of the location. The movement of the spare is the means to preserve and enrich the bases of the disposition of the Villette basin: it is the companion of the regular movement of the bridges and the locks of the canal.

5

6

Forum des Arènes

Design/Completion 1992/1994
Toulouse
M.T. Développement, S.C.E.T., C.L.F. Immo, S.A. H.L.M. les Chalets,
S.C.I.C. A.M.O., Le Nouveau Logis Méridional
35,000 square metres

Built after the Arènes High School, this was an important operation on more than one account. First because it is located on the outskirts of the greater Toulouse on the site of former railway wasteland and embodies the effort made to rehabilitate urban fringes and suburbs which is one of the major challenges of the end of this century. Second because the answer put forward is not an insipid regionalistic make-up job that clashes with the surroundings but an architectural project that comes to terms with its violent context and tries to create therewith lines of strength and a poetry, be it that of the fringes.

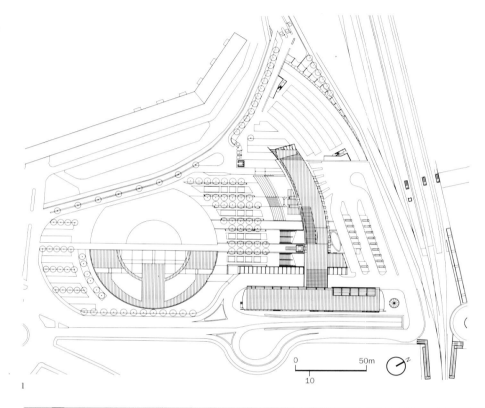

1

2

Despite a very limited budget, good use was made of the massive transport infrastructure (underground/railway station, bus/railway station, park-and-ride, road interchange), and of the complexity and overlapping of superstructure programmes (student residence, UNESCO international centre, low-cost housing, offices).

The whole is organised around the tension of two contradictory geometries born, one of the straight fault opened at the center of the school and multiplied into parallel paths, the other of the circularity of the Arenas of which the school retains the memory. The interior gives birth to a garden; the exterior is associated with the heavy infrastructures.

3

1   Block plan
2   Eastern frontage of apartment and office block
3   Northern frontage of bus station
4   View from 'trémie routière' on the Boulevard Koenigs

4

5

0   10m

The uncompromising aesthetic of the project draws its inspiration from road markings: alternately coloured strips, 'lacerations' and scoring of roads, route markings and night lighting, totems, etc. and becomes a screen and collages on the street, and staircases in the forum, visual gaps, tearings and grillwork in the parking.

But this aesthetic that allows the context to 'express' itself is balanced by the constitution of different, identifiable territories, by the clarity and ease with which the spaces may be understood, by the scale of the urban equipment and the way it was done (the organic structures of the bus stops' structures for example), by the night lighting. It is only in a contradictory space, that mirrors the social problems and paradoxes of this century that citizenship can be tempered, against exclusion and the extension of banality.

6

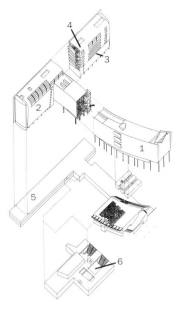

1 Aragon residence
2 UNESCO residence
3 Offices
4 Low cost housing
5 Parking
6 Underground station

7

8

9

10

11 Entrance to "Arènes" underground station
12 Detail
13 View of Forum from the Boulevard
14 Detail of car park entrance
15 Detail of northern frontage
16 Detail of underground car park
17 Arènes district seen from
the Boulevard Koenigs

11

12

13

14

15

16

17

18

19

18 Eastern frontage, seen by night
19 Boulevard Koenigs, by night
20 Seen by night

Jules Verne High School

Design/Completion 1991/1993
Cergy-le-Haut
Ile-de-France Regional Council
16,600 square metres

The Jules Verne High School is located at the outskirts of the new district of Cergy-le-Haut, at approximately thirty kilometres northwest of Paris in an environment yet still being urbanized. The land is triangular and bounded by two intersecting roads, one curved and the other rectilinear. This high school can accommodate 1,350 students and combines general courses and technical courses (production, electronics, metalworks).

This site and programme conditioned the architectural response with this project of two distinct but linked entities. The two teaching blocks are arranged along a composition and traffic axis which bisects the school grounds. The high school common areas (restaurant, resource centre, administration) are established along this axis.

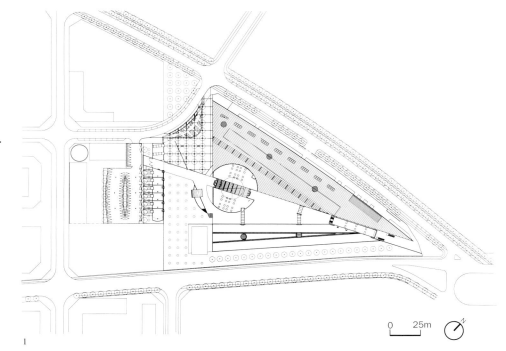

0   25m

1

2

1   Block plan
2   Night view of school life building with sculpture
    by Piotr Kowalski
3   Aerial view
4   Footbridge in inner courtyard

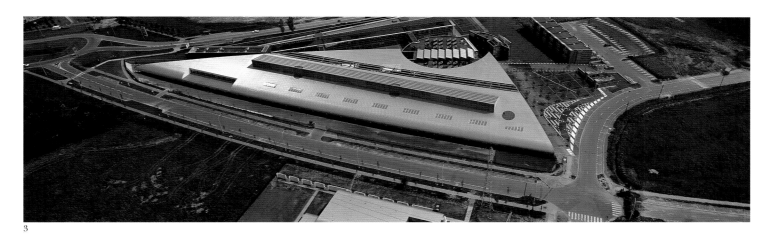

3

4

The technical block has a long curved facade that duplicates the curve of the road. The volumetry of this building is generated by curves subtended by a streamlined cross-section that integrates the workshops and technical classes. It is a product of technology. The general education block runs along the rectilinear road. The concrete screen facade is an expression of a building with urban characteristics, with priority being given to common internal volumes. High school life is organised around the common courtyard towards which all access roads converge and is punctuated in its center by Piotr Kowalski's glass hologram sculpture.

This high school celebrates its dedication to Jules Verne, tireless dreamer, inventor of stories that we still have pleasure reading today.

5

6

5 View of the access square
6 Inner courtyard
7 Aerial view
8 Cutaway, western side

7

9 View of the inner courtyard
10 Detail of painted concrete wall
11 Detail of inner space

9

10

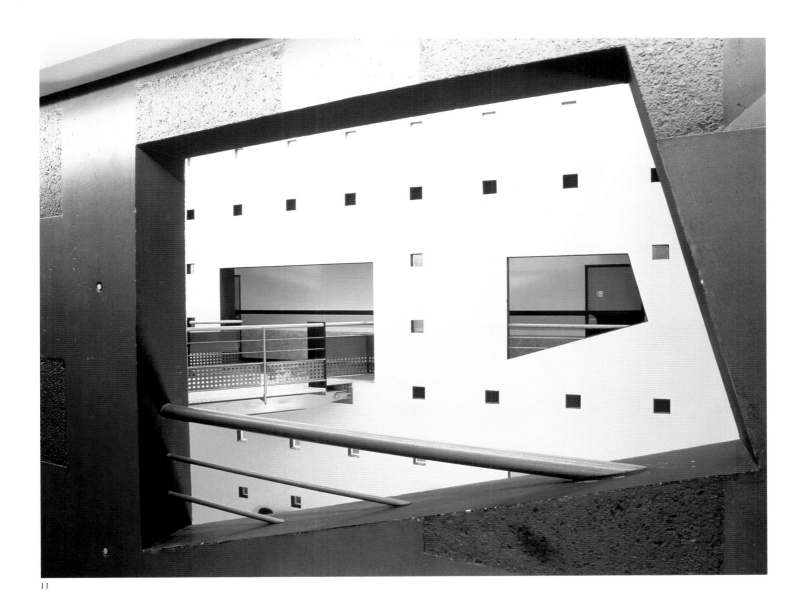

11

13

14 Black box (High school kitchen) on the east side
15 View of the facade from the courtyard of the technical building
16 Facade on the inner courtyard of the technical building

14

15

European Parliament

Design/Completion 1991/1997
Strasbourg
Société d'Exploitation de la Région Strasbourgeoise
180,000 square metres

The architecture of such a building must express the European culture and history. It must also be representative of our era and the democratic institution that supports it: a new heritage is being created which will take on its full value with the Euro-MPs' decisions.

The structure expresses the foundations of Western civilisation: Classicism and Baroque, from Galileo's circle to Kepler's ellipse, the passage from a centred geometrical structure (Galileo) to the anamorphosis (Borromini), the ellipse (Kepler, Gongora), an unstable moment in geometry, the passage from a central power to the democratic movement.

The European Parliament will be recognisable, identifiable, directly or through the transmission of images, and autonomous. It takes into account the morphology of the environment, from the city to Europe—the context in its broadest sense. These two notions, autonomy and context, are antinomic but are connected and complement one another.
Isn't modernity wanting contraries simultaneously?

This building has, at the same time, the strength of power and the openness of democracy.

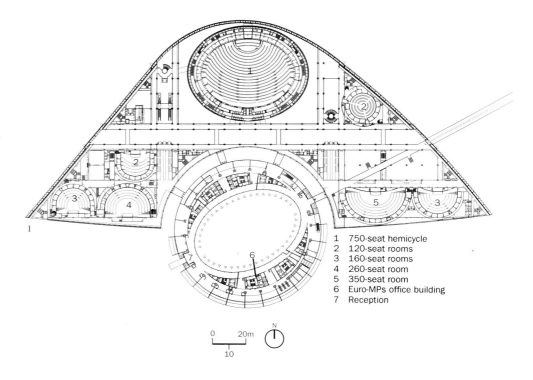

1
1   750-seat hemicycle
2   120-seat rooms
3   160-seat rooms
4   260-seat room
5   350-seat room
6   Euro-MPs office building
7   Reception

2

72

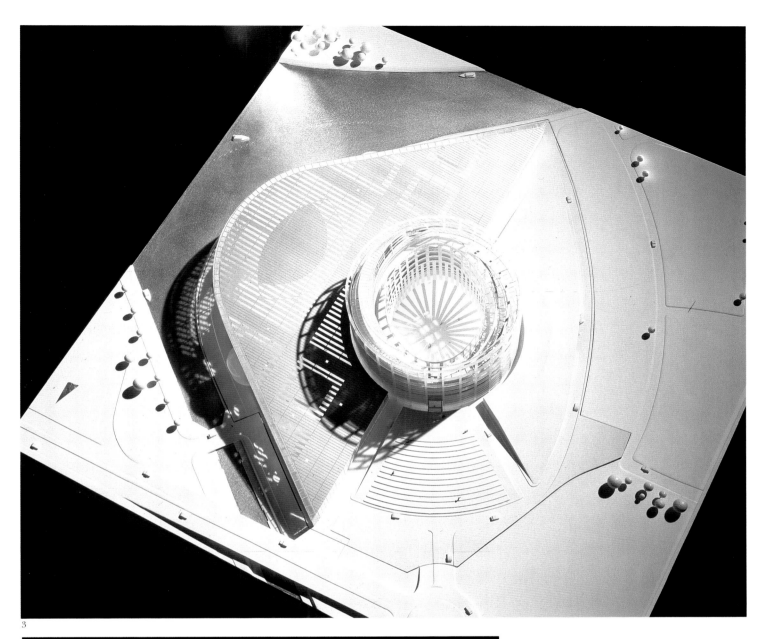

3

1 Plan of level +7.33
2 Photo of scale model showing (a) Council of Europe
  (b) Palace of Human Rights (c) Ungemach Garden City
3 Aerial view
4 General view

4

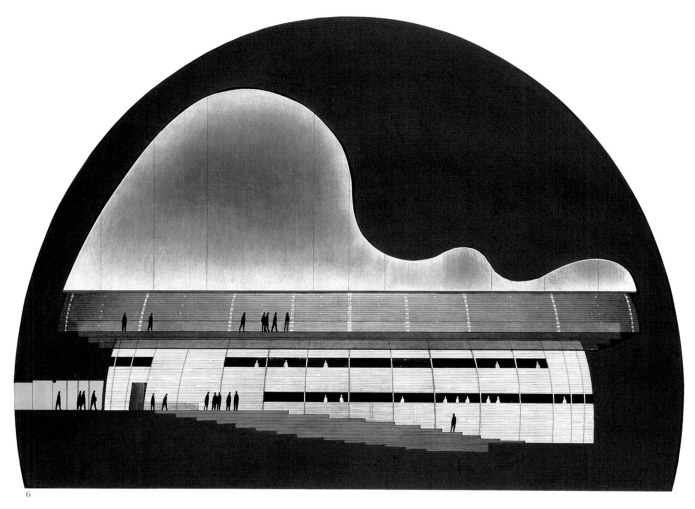

6

7

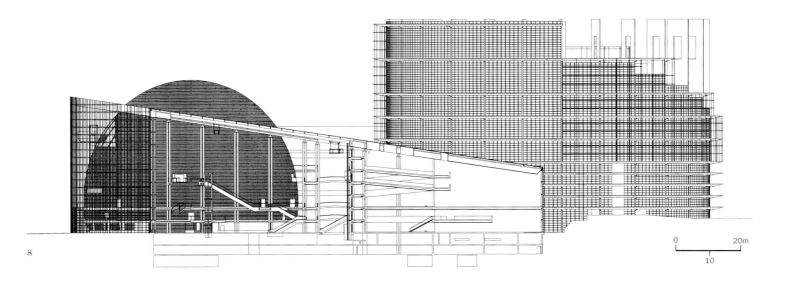

8

9

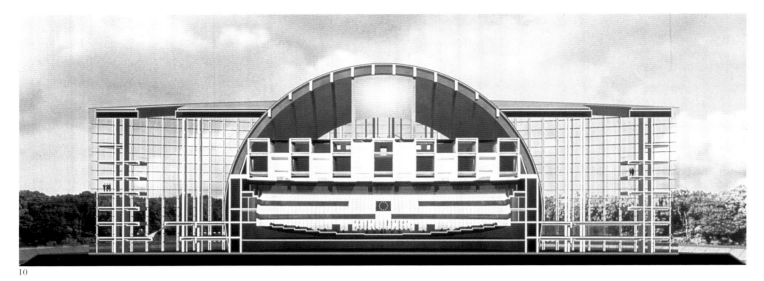

10

11

10 Cross-section
11 General interior view of the hemicycle
12 Detail of facade facing the river

European Parliame

University restaurant

Design/Completion 1990/1993
Dunkirk
Lille Education Authority, C.R.O.U.S.
1,500 square metres

Located close to the Citadel University, completed in 1990, the university restaurant presented an opportunity to express the city of Dunkirk's new tertiary vocation. This desire is expressed by a structure built on stilts, whose red colours and dynamic lines make it a contemporary building that can be identified from the city and that fits in with the surrounding harbour setting.

The building is joined to the Citadel islet context by a 'ground swell' sweeping through the structure on all levels. This part of the restaurant anchors the building to the urban structure. The 'ground swell' is located in the same line as the street with the university entrance, and channels the students towards the restaurant.

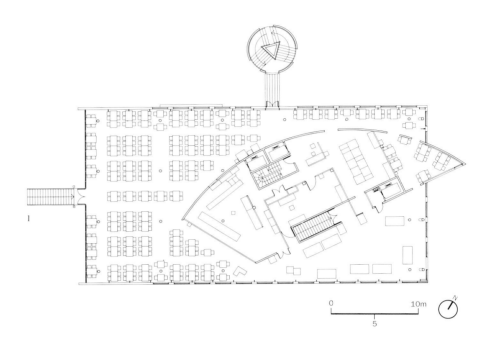

0   5   10m   N

1   University restaurant
2   University hub

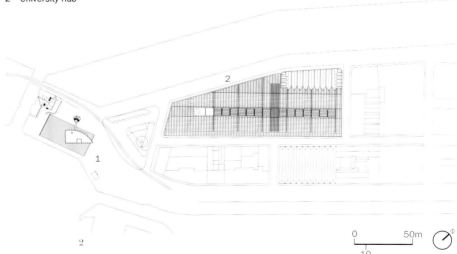

0   10   50m   N

2

3

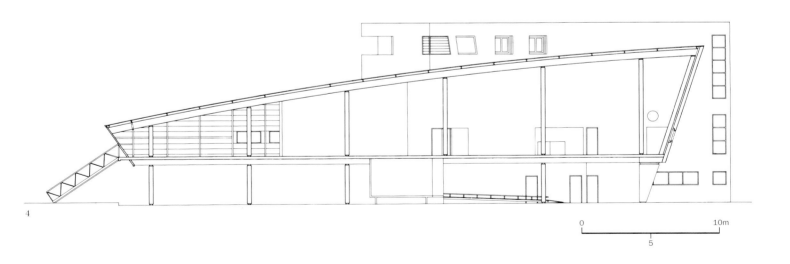

4

0   5   10m

1 First floor plan
2 Block plan
3 Southern frontage
4 Longitudinal section

The part built on stilts is located parallel to the banks of the bridge quays and frees the use of the embankment and the quays. The belvedere-like main building affords an exceptional view of the port of Dunkirk.

On this strategic site, the university restaurant is conceived as a signal, an urban event.

5

6

7

8

Apartment building and Jeanine Manuel Bilingual Active School

Design/Completion 1990/1994
Paris
S.E.M.E.A. XV, S.A.G.I.
9,000 square metres

The facade of the building can be described in terms of theatrical space such as a decor, a backdrop. The curtain falls in front of the facade, opening slightly to reveal a darker mass that evokes the focal point of the visual axis. By parting at the lower edge like a raised veil, this volume clears the vast portico of the entrance to the Bilingual Active School. The remainder of the facade, slightly in retreat from the street, blends in with the neighbouring buildings.

The school and apartments, are spatially and clearly situated and dissociated; the school, which has its own separate entrance, is located on the ground floor and organised around an atrium with a glass roof.

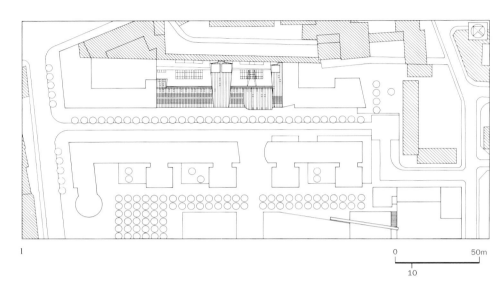

1

0   50m

10

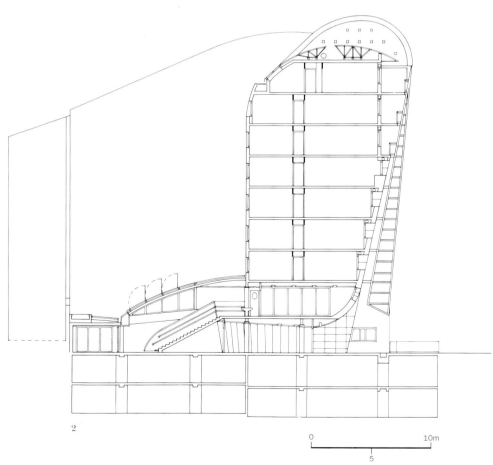

2

0   10m

5

3

1　Block plan
2　Cross-section
3　View from the south

4

The apartments occupy the upper stories, offering a vertical stacking of several types of dwelling, apartments in length on the first levels, and duplexes on the higher levels facing south towards the Edgar Faure street, freeing up space in the attic for technical control rooms without any structure jutting out from the roof.

The metal roof comes down the northern facade of the building like a very smooth skin.

5

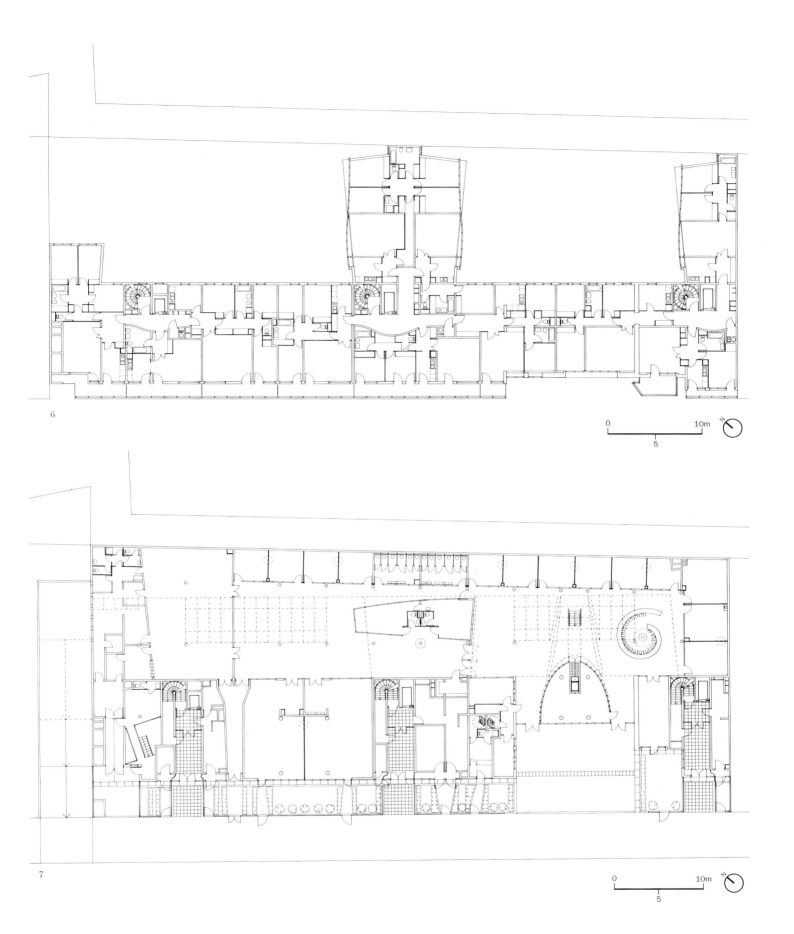

6

0   10m
|___|___|
     5

7

0   10m
|___|___|
     5

8 Detail of loggias on southern frontage
9 School central space
10 Southern frontage

8

9

Renault Technology Centre

Design 1990
Guyancourt
Régie Renault
550,000 square metres

The Renault consultancy made in 1990
was to draw up the 'general master plan' of
a structure capable of accommodating, by
the turn of the century, a very large and
highly complex technology centre, where
research, design and perfecting of the car
maker's production would be carried out.
Not quite architecture, since it was not just
a matter of erecting a building, but more
than mere town planning since the
prerequisite shapes, functions and volumes
had to be worked out. Such a large-scale
project, an industrial city, almost a
landscape, explicitly includes the element
of time. It could not consist of a 'turnkey'
megabuilding.

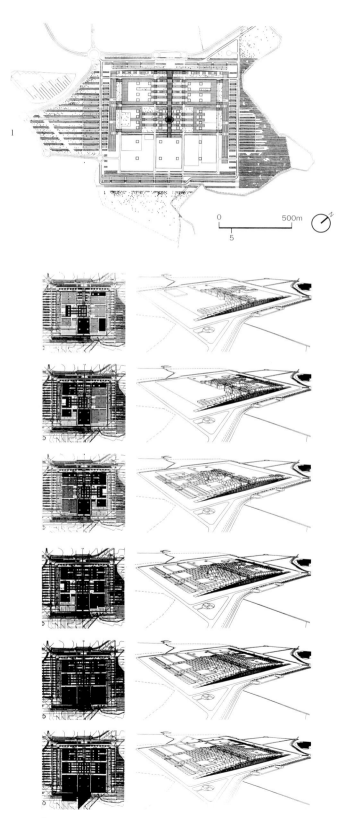

1

0   500m

5

2

1 Overall plan
2 Open-ended diagram
3 View of the 'beehive'
4 General view from the northwest
5 General view from the north

3

4

5

On the contrary, it was rather a question of establishing a land occupation procedure and managing it over time. Because of the scale and ambition of this project, it is possible to compare it to a city. Its building layout is that of a mixed urbanisation—tertiary sector, industry, services—that has its own logic, its templates, the movements and organisation of which are clearly defined.

For this project to rapidly anchor, adapt and evolve with time, strong elements are taken from the programme: irrigation and circulation axes, functional sets, nexuses, activity areas, personalized zones. They materialize a structure that simultaneously develops horizontally and vertically. A basis is created, vivified from the start by the construction of significant elements. The growth and extension scenarios are created from this basis. They use more or less space or density, depending on the needs, and welcome architecture's possibilities. They remain unified and use an unchanging template, a soft curve on the plains that writes the identity of the programme into the site.

6

7

6   Aerial view from the north
7   Detail of the roof
8   View of restaurant terrace
9   Perspective view of a patio

8

9

"Marché de l'Europe" business centre

Design 1990
Paris
Groupe Pierre 1er
25,000 square metres

A business centre in the heart of a
Haussmannian district, a rectangular islet
surrounded by four streets. Rehabilitation
pushed to the limit as an explicit encounter
between the city's memory and our time:
the renovation of the "Marché de l'Europe",
which houses offices, neighbourhood
amenities and an undercover market. The
structural components of the carcass have
been preserved. The building is wrapped
in a sheet of glass carried by a secondary
structure that completes the bearing
structure. It is topped by a glass dome roof
that duplicates the layout and rounded
shape of Haussmannian buildings. At street
level, set-backs express the public nature of
the program: daycare, market and municipal
services. A covered public walkway crosses
the islet, in the Paris tradition. This project
is in keeping with a dialectic between a
certain form of the city's memory and an
expression of today's technical culture.

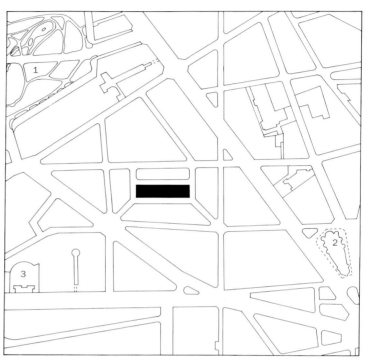

1 Monceau park
2 Saint Augustin Church
3 Jacquemart-André Museum

1

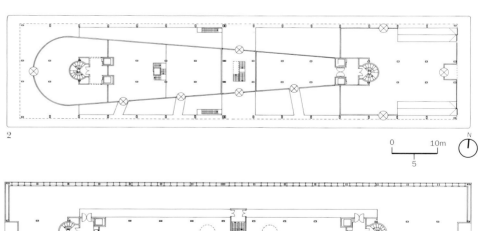

2

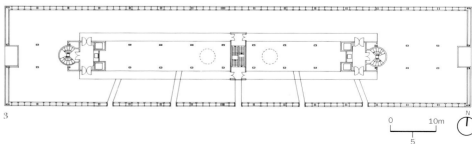

3

94

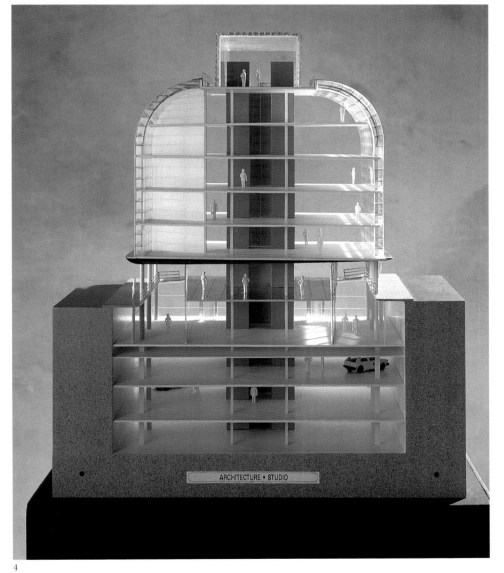

1 Location plan
2 Ground floor plan
3 Fourth floor plan
4 Cross-section
5 Aerial view
6 Rue Treillard frontage

4

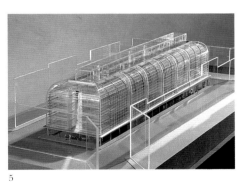

5

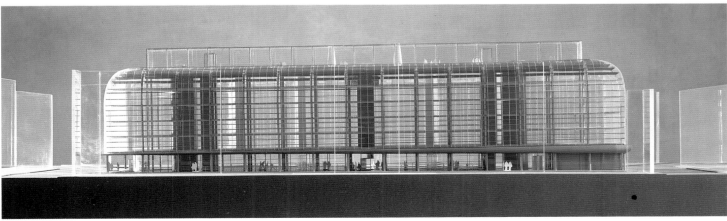

6

Doctor's surgery

Design/Completion 1990/1991
Lagny sur Marne
Docteur FX. Sallée
120 square metres

The surgery was built for an endocrinologist and three paediatricians in the garden of Doctors Aliette and Francois-Xavier Sallée's residence. It fits in with the homogeneous low-rise structures overlooking the Marne river.

The only restrictions imposed by the clients were aimed at preserving the privacy of the consulting rooms and the family home. In contrast to the neighbouring low-rise dwellings, our approach consisted in occupying and structuring all the land available. The efficient volume was divided diagonally into two sections, one built-up, the other without any building in order to preserve the existing trees.

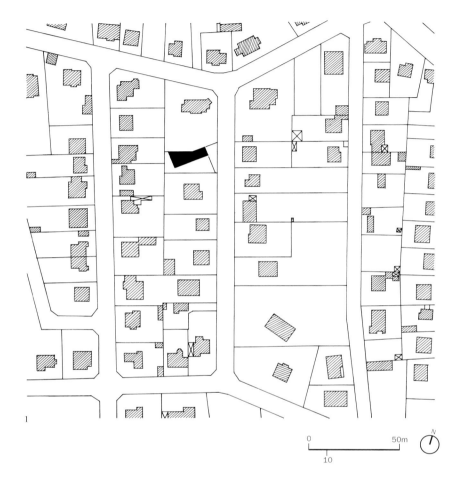

1

0   10   50m   N

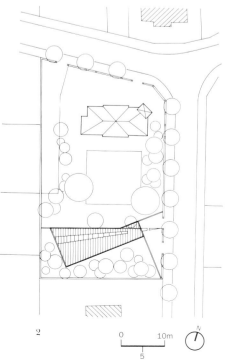

2

0   5   10m   N

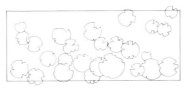

(a) Area covered by building

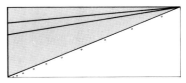

(d) Bundles

1 Location plan
2 Block plan
3 Conceptual diagram
4 Southern frontage, seen by night

(b) Mineral/Vegetable

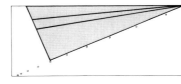

(e) Frame

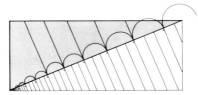

(c) Layout grid continues No.1: Numbers 60+

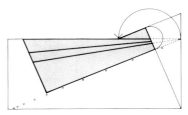

(f) Rotation/Entrance

3

4

The internal functioning is organised according to three angular bundles using distinctive materials, colours and light qualities: services—waiting room/traffic/consulting rooms. The waiting 'caves', in particular, give rise to all kinds of games.

Accent is put on the perspectives by a variable structural template of continuous progression. The spatial anamorphosis mirrors the evolution of children's perception of their relationship with environment and adults. Intimacy is guaranteed by a selective approach to the surroundings, as in the dissociation of the facades' two functions 'view' and 'light'. The tip of the building pivots in the garden in order to clear, behind the existing grit stone wall, an entrance defined by opalescent glass panels.

5

5   View of building in the garden
6   Southern frontage
7   Southern frontage, seen by night

6

7

Cayenne-Rochambeau airport

Design/Completion 1989/1996
Cayenne, French Guiana
Cayenne Chamber of Commerce and Industry
8,600 square metres

A major challenge for the city of Cayenne, this project, in addition to trebling the existing surface, revitalises the aerodrome and asserts its duality between the continental roots and the booming satellite launcher market. Thus, a veritable industrial zone has been created, that will soon be able to accommodate a million passengers, a prestige tool in the centre of the Guianan economy. The building is double-layered in the new airport tradition, thus offering maximum transparence and convergence between the plane and the car. The building system is simple, clear and high-tech, through the use of high-performance materials and resources. The roof is a rigging facade turned towards the sky; the structure expresses a present-day poetry, the inner hooding glorifies accuracy.

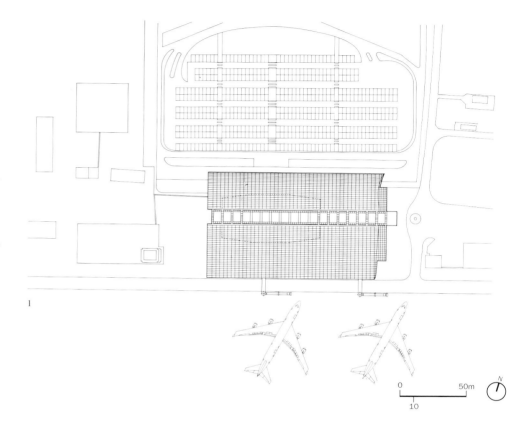

1

2

1   Block plan
2   Interior perspective
3   Cross-section

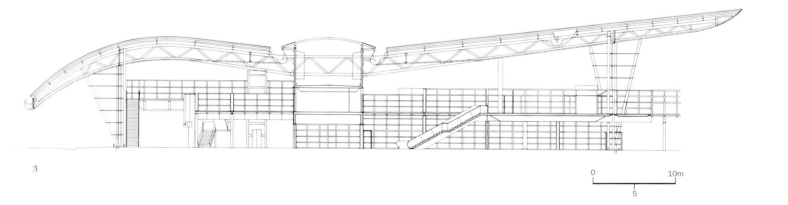

3

0   10m

5

Arènes High School

Design/Completion 1989/1991
Toulouse
Midi-Pyrénées Region
15,000 square metres

In 1988 the Midi-Pyrénées Region initiated a competition for the construction of a communications high school. The surrounding urban landscape, discontinuous is dominated by the imposing 'cristal' bar that modern urbanism left. The concept of the Arènes Communications High School is structured by the emblematic figure of the quarter: the Golden Sun Arena that was built after the war. This Arena occupied the whole site and the area originally covered has been preserved exactly, thus giving the project a contextual permanence, a scenographic space linking the high school to the city.

The diameter, like a geological fault, defines an axis from which to start the new district and the facade, entirely metallic, conceived like a technical grid, is visibly the screen for the communicating activities of the school.

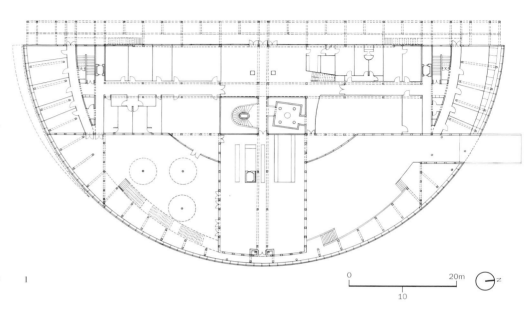

1

2

1   Ground floor plan
2   Block plan
3   Evolution of construction
4   Seen by night
5   View of inner courtyard

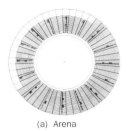
(a) Arena

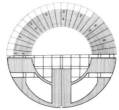
(b) High School and
Arena

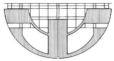
(c) High School

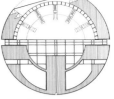
(d) High School and
Communications house

3

4

5

This autonomous object thereby answers its immediate surroundings, but defuses the modern paradigm and redefines its territory as a fabric and rearticulates it to the city. In the high school, the vanished circle is recreated, retranscribed, distanced; the geometry of its arcs is combined with the orthogonal geometry peculiar to teaching institutions. The overall volume is indented by terraces, patios, belvederes, a series of set-backs that establish physical links and prospects on urban layouts. These directions—circle, orthogonality, site data—impact on each other and create a third reading order that belongs by rights to the site we are creating; the complexity of the spaces harmonises with the apparent simplicity of the form.

6

7

8

9

11

10 Brightness of light in the passageways
11 View of inner courtyard from passageways

12 View of passageway
13 Western frontage, seen by night
14 View of staircase

12

13

14

Scenography for the "Paris and the daguerreotype" exhibition

Design/Completion 1989/1989
Carnavalet museum, Paris
City of Paris Directorate of Cultural Affairs

The concept for the production of this exhibition was faced with the major difficulty presented by daguerreotypes, which are small and fragile. Viewing daguerreotypes requires appropriate lighting to eliminate the mirror effect of the plate, and an accurate angle of sight.

The exhibition opens on to a large gallery with black walls. The shape of the walls, the slope of the floor and the ceiling conjure up the convergence of light beams. At both ends of the gallery, two blown-up details of daguerreotypes answer one another. Differently shaped windows enable the visitor to discover the daguerreotypes placed behind the walls.

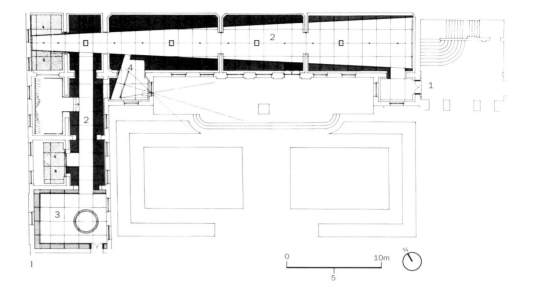

1   Entrance
2   Ancient daguerreotypes
3   Modern daguerreotypes
4   Black room

1   Ground floor plan
2   Daguerreotype presentation gallery, seen from the entrance

2

A few portholes provide virtual escapes into the garden, emphasising the real/virtual image opposition. Thus the tonality of the exhibition is deliberately dark to promote the viewing of the displayed works and to eliminate reflections. The mood lighting is achieved by the blue-tinged glow of the video monitors. Thus the daguerreotype, which marks the invention of photography 150 years ago, is symbolically lit by the carrier of today's images.

3

3   Detail of a gallery wall
4   Daguerreotype presentation gallery

4

European Patents Office

Design 1989
The Hague, Netherlands
200,000 square metres

Scientific and technical discoveries are often born of meditations on nature or ordinary and extraordinary events of live.

Far from conceiving the European Patents Office building as an independent whole living solely off its technological fantasies, we wished to relate it to its surroundings by a system that envelops, appropriates and reinterprets.

The proposed site in The Hague is a large park criss-crossed by canals. The European Patents Office is a glass parallelepiped, surrounded by water, with a square base measuring 180 metres along each side. It fits in with an orthogonal rational layout grid oriented by the city which restricts the land as a whole.

The natural part, which is thus distanced and absorbed, implants the progressionist utopia in its terrestrial memory and in time: a reminder of its origins and the intangible laws of the physical world. But in addition to creating a microclimate, this 'capture' permits all possible reconstructions and the enlargement of the relational geographical context to include a universal dimension.

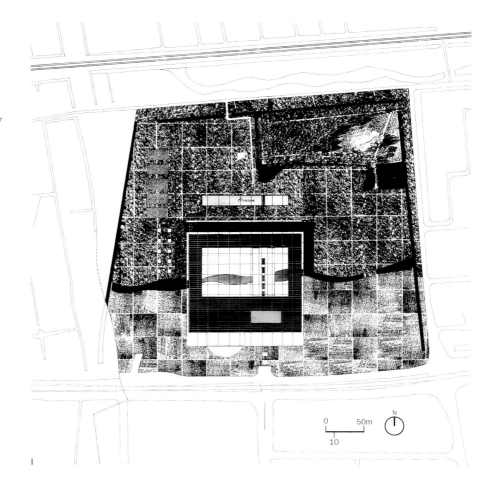

1

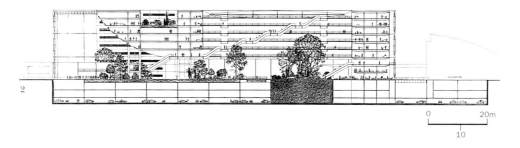

2

3

The building offers its own innovations: facade panels with variable opaqueness liquid crystals, a technology of relation and confidentiality. Technology is thus considered not as an end in itself but as the vector of a particular poetics.

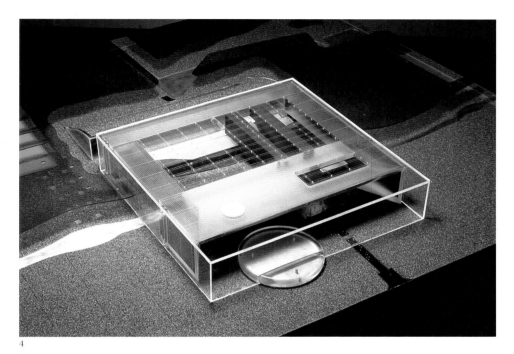

4

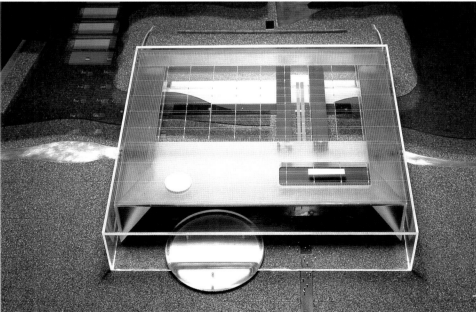

5

1   Block plan
2   Cross-section
3   Entrance frontage
4   Aerial view
5   View from the south

University residence

Design/Completion 1989/1996
Paris
S.A.G.I.
11,000 square metres

Framing what one wishes to see, shielding from what one does not want to suffer: that is the challenge facing this 340 student studio project built right on the edge of the ring road. On the ring road side, noise, speed: a curved wall, a shield 30 by 100 metres, like a giant screen, a signal built into the kinetic landscape of the city as seen from a motor car. On the Paris side, a quiet, green belt: three curved, 11-level tips pressing against the shield. All the studio flats are located in these three south-facing tips; at the points and in the centre, large collective volumes complete the private spaces by 20 square metre rooms. The shield is double, it protects from the noise, clings closely to the traffic; it is also a Piranesian walkway with views of the cars whirling round and of the suburban horizon.

It uses 'peri-urban' vocabulary: asphalt, light, advertising. From the dwellings, it is transparency, modern comfort, living space.

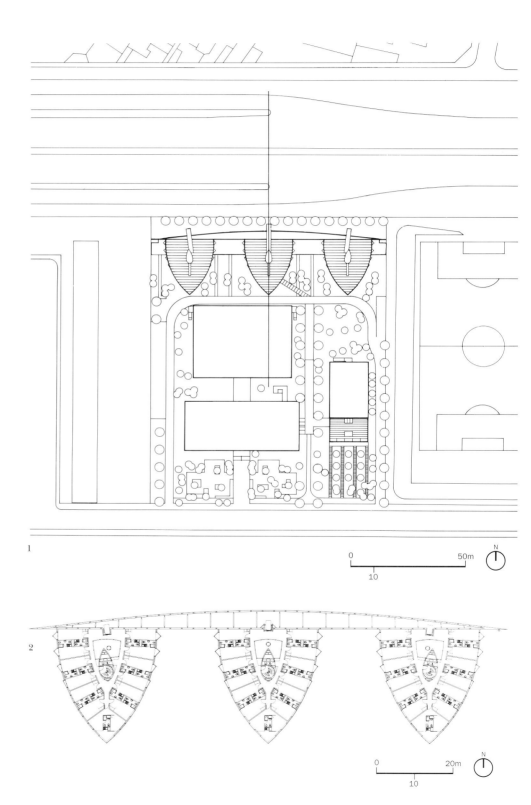

1

0   10   50m   N

2

0   10   20m   N

3

4

1   Block plan
2   Stock floor plan
3   Park section
4   Northern frontage
5   General view
6   Southern frontage

5

6

"La City" business centre

Design/Completion 1988/2000
Besançon
Doubs Department Road and Building Infrastructure Corporation
35,000 square metres

Besançon was the home of the first great collectivist utopias of the industrial era, of which the phalansteries that grouped complementary activities—housing, work, services—in a large-scale built entity. A social culture expressed into architecture, a topographical context perceived as obvious by Architecture Studio.

An award winner in the 1988 international competition, Architecture Studio started Phase 1 of the site in 1991, grouping together 15,000 square metres of cabled, telecomputerised offices, a foreign language training centre, a hotel, apartments, the head office of a bank.

1

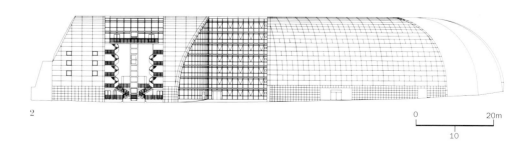

2

118

1 Block plan
2 View from the quays
3 Ground floor plan
4 Southern side wall
5 Operation diagram

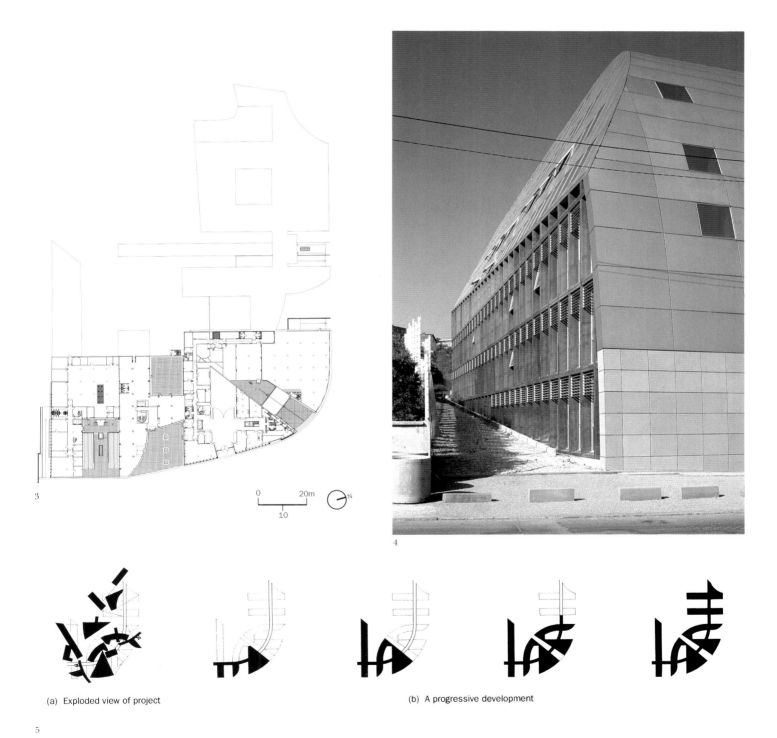

3

0   10   20m

N

4

(a) Exploded view of project

(b) A progressive development

5

On this site, located on the bank of the Doubs River and dominated by powerful slopes mastered by Vauban's architecture, the roof is treated as a sign, a unified cover, curved without a break down to ground level, marking the periphery of a virtual dome, a dome fractured by deep cuts corresponding to the facades of the buildings. The meeting of two characteristic geometries, the curve of the cover and the verticality of the facades generate a third geometry of atypical logic. It weaves relations of continuity with the streets, axes, orientations, topography and the templates of waterfront buildings. This unified complex is a veritable piece of city.

6

6   Block plan
7   Detail of the fault

"La City" business centre   121

8

9

122

10

11 View of gable and eastern facade
12 View from the quays
13 City view
14 View from the north

11

12

13

Student living centre

Design/Completion 1988/1989
Parc du Futuroscope, Jaunay-Clan
O.P.D.H.L.M. Vienne Department
4,500 square metres

Completed in 1989, the student living centre
is located within the Parc du Futuroscope.
These so-called 'experimental' dwellings
are computerised and connected to
databanks. They have been designed as
easily identifiable prototypes of a mode of
living that reflects our changing society.
The movable and immovable elements are
adapted to facilitate the use of these
services: cabled network accessible from
multiple points, mobile shelf-staircase
designed as the central connection point
for the studio flats. The residence built in
the fields is modest and user-friendly.
Small clusters of several studios distributed
by a spinal circulation system are arranged
in a semicircle, with galleries connecting
them to the shared services in the centre of
the ground. Echoing the High School of
the Future, the dwellings retain an industrial
language while at the same time showing
that they are not robot boxes but houses,
with colours, room, light, people.

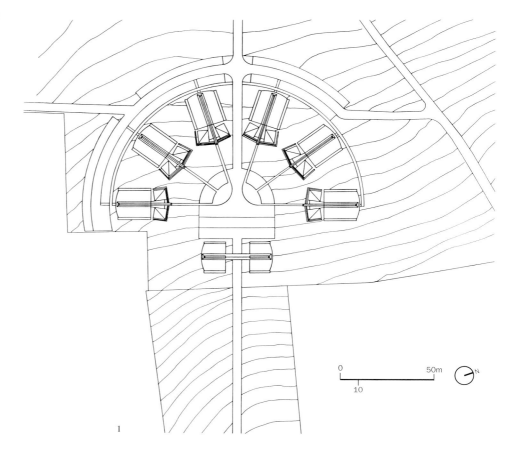

1

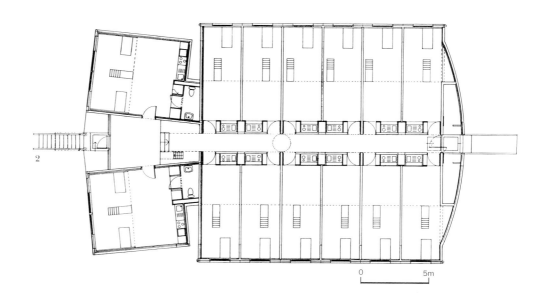

2

126

1 Block plan
2 Ground floor plan
3 Cross-section
4 Passageway to accommodation

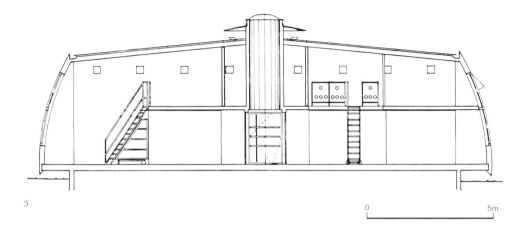

3

0   5m

4

5

6

7

5 Detail of stairs
6 Circulation servicing the accomodation
7 Stairs to the access terrace
8 Detail of the frontage
9 View of accommodation blocks

8

9

Canal+ headquarters

Design 1988
Paris
Canal+, Cogedim
35,000 square metres

A project with an exceptional programme, the headquarters of a television chain, a request by the clients for a strong and contemporary image, a plot by the Seine. Extreme conditions where reputedly contradictory forces are conjugated: respect for the context and inventiveness.

A unified, autonomous, atypical shape, neither a high-rise on a parcel nor a building with street frontage nor an islet; as much as possible of the land is taken up by the building. Its limits, in surface and in volume, are those imposed by the city, there is hardly any change of emphasis; an urban organism is born. Its dependency towards the city generates its unexpected body. The facade/roof system is replaced by a continuous shell—black, metal, mysterious. The fractures, openings, traffics are determined by the inner functioning, an autonomous vocabulary.

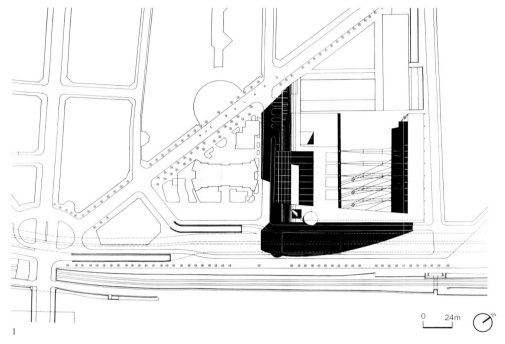

0 24m

1

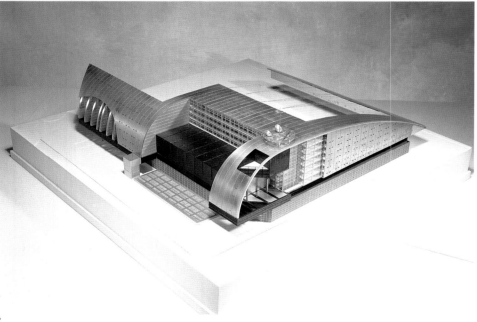

2

1 Block plan
2 Aerial view
3 Cross-section
4 View from the south
5 Entrance facade
6 Frontage on the Seine

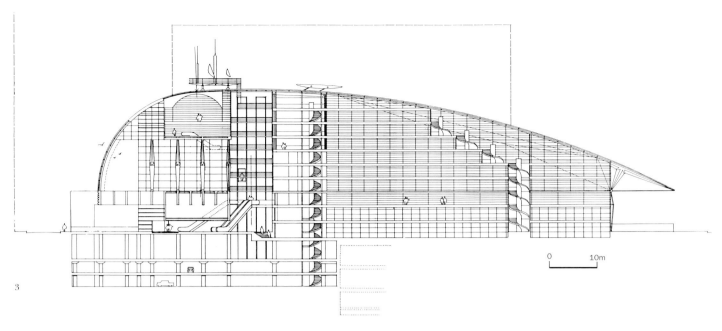

3

4

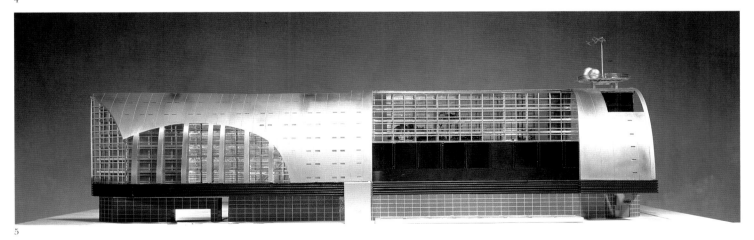

5

6

National Judo Institute

Design/Completion 1988/1996
Paris
French Judo Federation
34,000 square metres

Accurate and smooth, the National Judo Institute is an 'object' placed near the ring road, between Paris and its suburbs, in that interval where the breaks and contortions of the city—signs of life—are expressed. A dome of tarnished copper, tense, low, the project expresses a soft geometry, a portion of a sphere abruptly stopped by the block boundaries on the ring road side. The cutting-up of a simple shape by irregular boundaries produces these diverse faces, obvious paradoxes of geometry.

Under the arched beams of the dome, with a wingspan of 100 metres, is the dojo, judo stadium for 3000 spectators and training rooms. The linear building houses the head office of the National Judo Federation and other sporting federations, offices and a hotel. Between the two, a covered street where a rough concrete wall confronts openings towards the dojo.

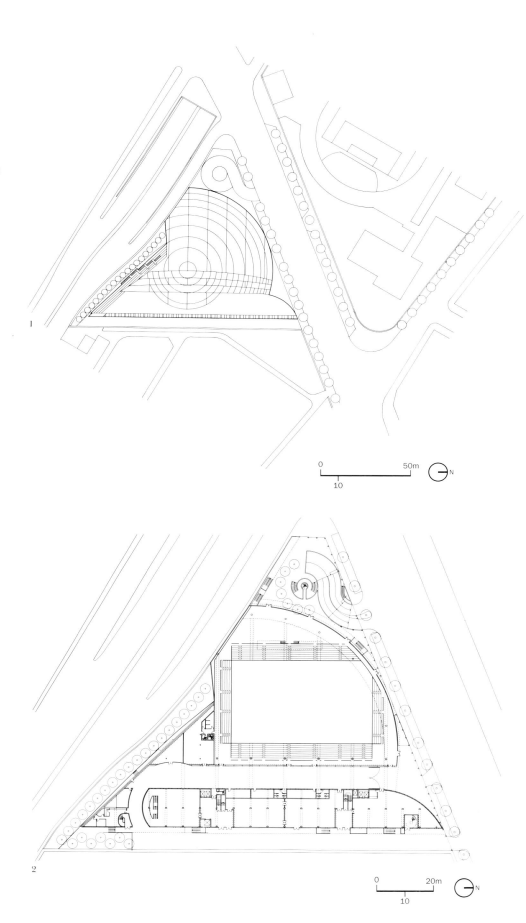

1 Block plan
2 Upper level ground floor plan
3 Cross-sectional elevation
4 View from the north
5 View from the northeast
6 View from the south

3

0   20m
  10

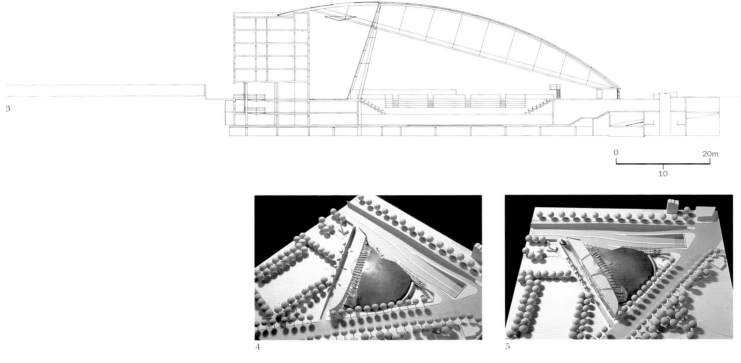

4

5

6

Post office and mail sorting centre

Design/Completion 1988/1993
Paris
Paris-Nord Post Office Directorate
11,000 square metres

Dominated by the metal structures of the Boulevard de la Chapelle elevated railway, the building set out to sew up the urban fabric. Its fragmentation into three volumes that are clearly dissociated and individualised in their architectural treatment is a response to the exploded morphology of the context as well as the complexity of its programme.

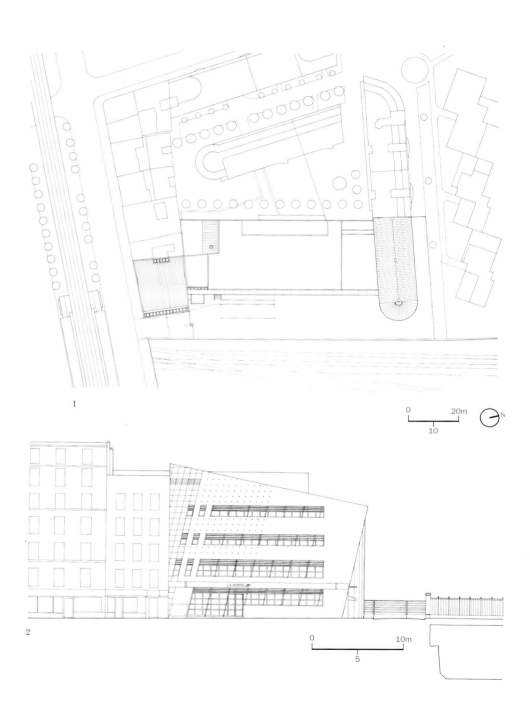

1

0   10   20m

2

0   5   10m

1 Block plan
2 Boulevard de la Chapelle frontage
3 Detail of Boulevard de la Chapelle frontage
4 Eastern frontage

3

4

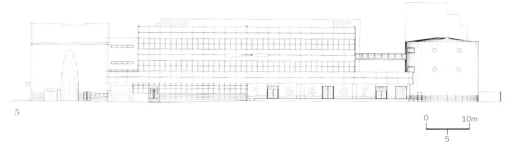

5

0   10m

5

On the Boulevard, the administrative building and the post office, as well as the concourse centre at the far end of the block, extend existing volumetries. They are linked to the sorting centre and its transfer area. The main facade faces the goods station and reveals itself to restless city dwellers through catenaries, cables, railings and structures. The emblematic colours of the post office, yellow and blue, wink at this destructured kinetic perception, in playful contrast to the black building on the Boulevard, which is dislodged, shifted out of its environment, ripped open by the shaft of its staircase.

The metallic cladding, the lights and the relentless ballet of trucks night and day comfort the image of an openly industrial building in the center of Paris.

6

5   Facade facing the railway tracks
6   Frontage on the boulevard
7–8   Inside the mail sorting room

7

8

9

10

9 View from the railway track
10 View under viaduct of overhead line
   of Paris underground
11 Night view
12 View from the Boulevard de la Chapelle

11

12

Fire station

Design/Completion 1988/1995
Gennevilliers
City of Paris, Police Headquarters
12,000 square metres

The fire station inscribes its complex programme in the scattered suburban environment: the firemen's accommodation, the telephone exchange, the exercise tower, some offices. On this site which lacks togetherness, the fire station introduces drama, a meaningful opposition.

At the bow, the articulation of two buildings designed to match each other. One of them leans forward, the other straightens up; one submits, the other swaggers about; one slides, the other flies off. It is a necessary choreographic figure: the mastery of alignments.

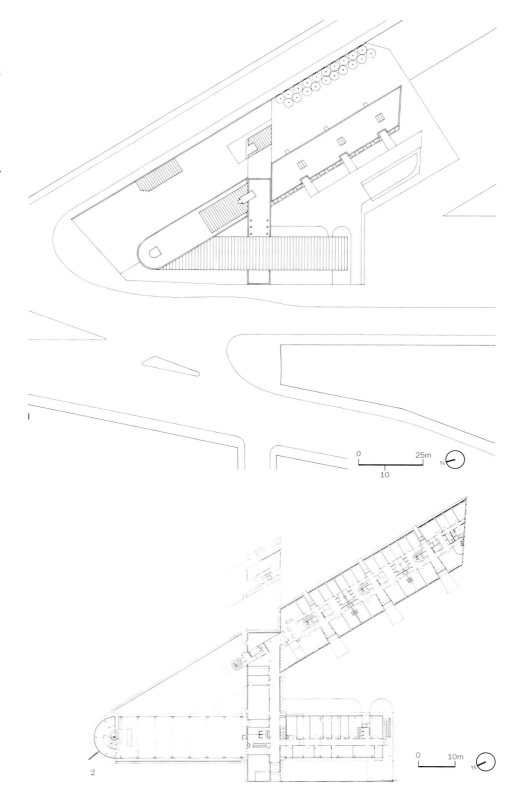

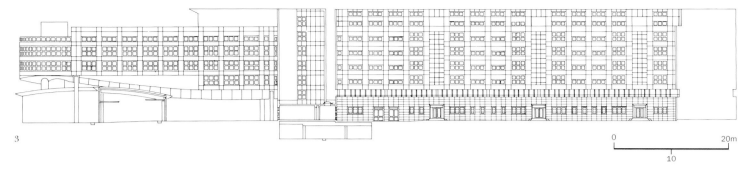

3

0
10
20m

1 Block plan
2 First floor plan
3–4 Western frontage
5 Detail of western frontage

4

5

On the flank, a third figure is introduced which upsets this harmony. The battering ram makes a hole and extracts an unpredictable element from it. Detached, dissymmetrical, almost unbalanced, the instruction tower advances into the limelight and reveals gable walls. The colours contribute to the contrapuntal writing of the architectural project. Therefore they constitute neither an analysis nor a comparison. Like the architectural shape, the colours assert the buildings, not as singular entities, but as figures of a set.

6

7

8

6   Eastern frontage
7   Detail of administration southern side wall
8   Detail of western frontage
9   Exercise tower in front of accommodation block

9

Citadel University

Design/Completion 1987/1990
Dunkirk
Dunkirk Urban Community
15,000 square metres

The Citadel University, completed in 1990, takes an active place in the landscape, or rather in an industrial geography: on the quay, a pier of Citadel Island. The allocated land included a former tobacco warehouse, symbolic of a harbour. The whole plot has been taken over; the aluminium roof, a smooth, unified cowling whose grey colour changes with the shades of the sky, curves down towards the street, on the city side. Seen from that side, it appears between the old buildings, metal line, curve upon a line in time, with an apparently different speed. On the harbour side, the facade resumes the alignment and template of the context, and something of its texture: it is covered in brick-coloured industrialised elements.

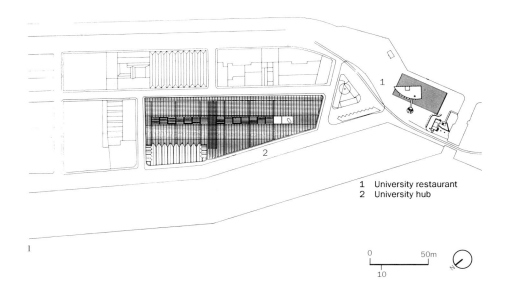

1   University restaurant
2   University hub

1

0   50m
   10

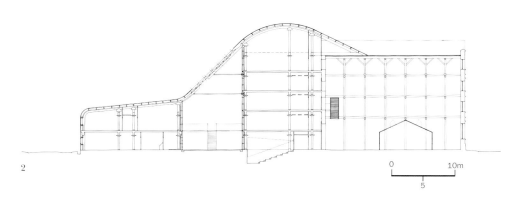

2

0   10m
   5

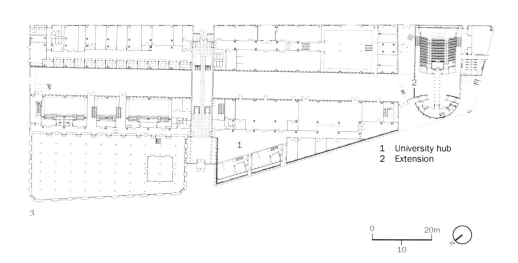

3

1   University hub
2   Extension

0   20m
   10

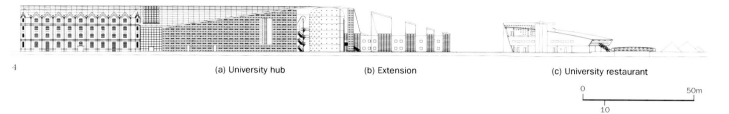

4

(a) University hub   (b) Extension   (c) University restaurant

0   50m
10

5

1   Block plan
2   Section of old warehouses
3   Ground floor plan
4   Quay frontage
5   Aerial view

The meeting of geometries that are deliberately foreign to each other— the vertical plane of the facade, the old warehouse complex with its crenellated roof and the metal wave—creates other geometries. Inside, the warehouse is stripped, its woodwork and the reverse of the old walls visibly repaired: it becomes a covered square. A street used to cross the site, its route remains in the glass roof that cuts the building at right angles. The extension of the buildings is currently taking place.

6

6–7 Detail of the roof
  8 Detail of circulation

7

8

9 Detail of eastern frontage
10 Inner street
11 Detail of quay frontage
12 The city seen through the sunbreakers

9

10

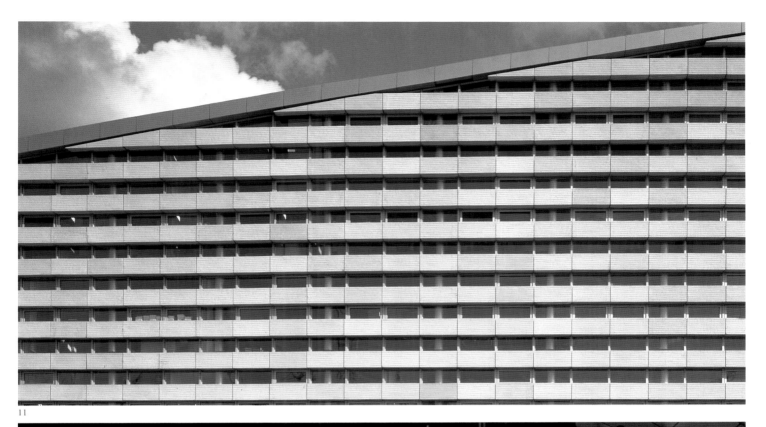

11

12

13

14

15

16

17

18

19

20

21

22

23

French Embassy

Design/Completion 1986/1989
Muscat, Sultanate of Oman
Ministry of Foreign Affairs
4,600 square metres

Seaside, edge of the Sultanate of Oman desert, relentless sun, a site where all remains to be invented, shade most of all. In Muscat the embassy district is made up of rectangular 180x80 metre lots. The building is contemporary, with references to the Arab tradition and to the national requirement of its preservation. Monument of an institution, it asserts it and also reveals qualities of softness, shadow and light, the privacy of a palace. Nearly all the land is covered by a perforated concrete grid, horizontal transposition of a *moucharabieh*.

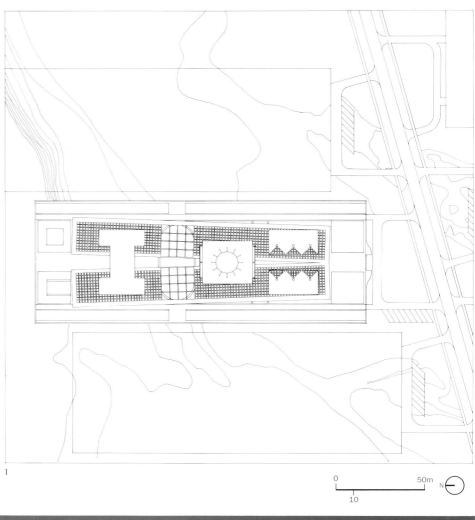

1

2

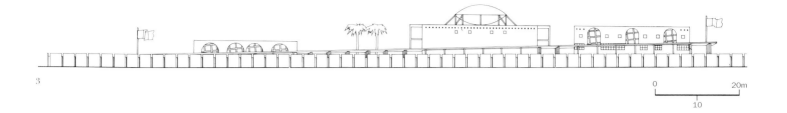

1   Block plan
2   Detail of entry
3   Western frontage
4   Entrance esplanade
5   View of the second garden

From this inclined cover emerge the buildings of ambassador's residency and the chancellery crowned by a cupola. The slope of the *moucharabieh* warps perspectives, a device amplified by the leaning grid that divides the windows into arcades on the upper level. Underneath, an untreated concrete colonnade, a monochrome half-light spattered with the bright colours diffused by stained glass windows. In the middle, the grid is broken lengthwise, concentrating the spectacular point of view on the main axis. A long basin accompanies the perspective that evokes the *faljah*, the trickle of water that refreshes palaces and gardens; it collects the streaming water on the *moucharabieh*.

The water, charoscure and air flow create a natural air conditioning at ground level, while the upper levels of the buildings are roughly chiselled, dazzlingly white marble in the burning light.

6

7

8

9

6   Space under dome
7   Passageway under the dome
8   Shadows of the *moucharabieh*
9   Space under the *moucharabieh*

10

11

12

13

10 Underface of dome
11 Shadows under the *moucharabieh*
12 Detail of the eastern frontage
13 View of the northern frontage from the sea
14 View of the southwest angle
15 Emergence of chancery
16 View of the sea

14

15

16

17 The second courtyard
18 View of the first courtyard
19 The pool, seen by night
20 The second courtyard, seen by night

17

18

19

20

Our Lady of the Ark of the Covenant Church

Design/Completion 1986/1996
Paris
Diocesan Association of Paris, Archbishopric of Paris
1,400 square metres

The dedication of Our Lady of the Ark of the Covenant implies the whole theology of the relationship between the Old and the New Testament in an architecture that expresses this theology, while at the same time experiencing its own constraints.

First of all, the church symbolises the Ark of the Old Alliance. A perfect volume was selected, that of the cube, because of its simplicity; from a symbolic point of view, this shape is immediately interpretable and is faithful not to archaeological accuracy—the biblical Ark was a parallelepiped—but to the intended meaning: the equal sides of the cube reflect the presence of the one and only.

This shape is inserted in a tridimensional metal grid that circumscribes a volume, creates a transition between the secular world and the sanctuary, vertically transposes an ancient narthex, guides the eye vertically up to the bell-tower and signals to the centre of town.

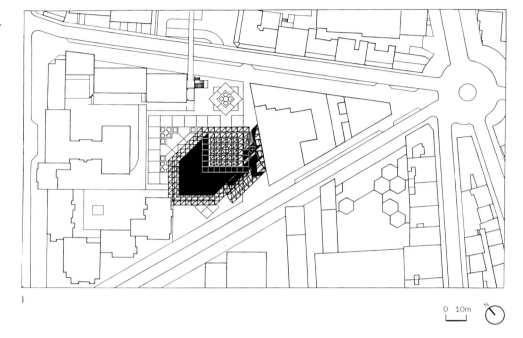

1

0 10m

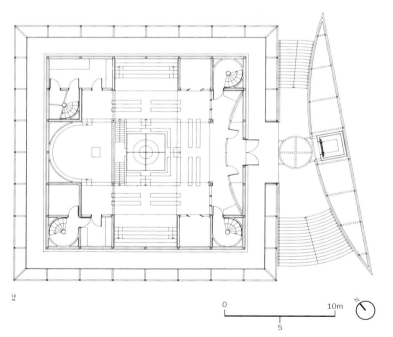

2

0   10m

5

1 Block plan
2 First floor plan
3 Aerial view, seen by night
4 Northern frontage

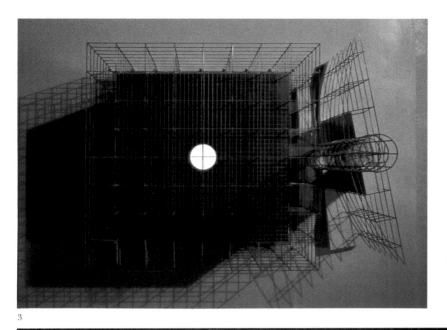

3

4

The twelve foundation pillars refer both to the twelve tribes united in their obedience to the law and to the twelve apostles of the new Israel.

From the main entrance, everything leads the faithful to the immutable rock, a central figure of Christ, and to his body sheltered in the heart of the Ark which irradiates the whole space like that of the tabernacle.

Through the centering of the cross, through the light from the stained glass windows—on which the Decalogue and John's Prologue are engraved face to face—through the play of volumes, the gathering is marked by the seal of the Cross. The eyes converge towards the high altar: from the gallery to the oratory, everything is governed by this point where the ceiling recesses, which vertically reflect, modify and amplify this cruciform plan, continually direct to the axis of the choir, to the one and only celestial treasure.

5

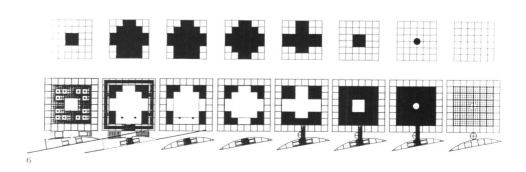

6

7

5   Entrance way
6   Cubic break-up
7   Longitudinal cross-section

Finally, the high altar occupies a central and predominant position: it looks over the hollow of the crypt and the inner tiers of the oratory, and combines, without the unicity of the eucharistic centre ever being affected, with the tabernacle of the eucharistic reserve in front of which it will be possible to continually meditate on the reality thus offered to the heart of the world in the ascending movement made of light which is suggested by the zenithal occulus.

This completes the movement that makes the whole structure into a new ark, a large tabernacle of the incarnate word.

8

8   Northern frontage
9   Cross-section

9

High School of the Future

Design/Completion 1986/1987
Jaunay-Clan
Poitou-Charentes Region
19,000 square metres

The High School of the Future is situated near Poitiers, in the Parc du Futuroscope; here the rural geographical context fades away and lets the park take over: a technological imagery. A metal-clad triangle, the high school is positioned within a discontinuous collection of signal-objects that finally form a whole, through a kind of play consensus. It apparently has the unequivocal simplicity of a giant toy: a kind of plane. It looks light, its external walls visibly have no thickness: curtain-wall, aluminium-leaf roof, recessed structure, as if they were alien, taking root. The heart of the triangle, its centre of gravity, is an elliptical courtyard surrounded by a concrete grid with red streaks. A mechanism sets a flying wing in motion, a piece of building moves and provides a roof for this inner courtyard.

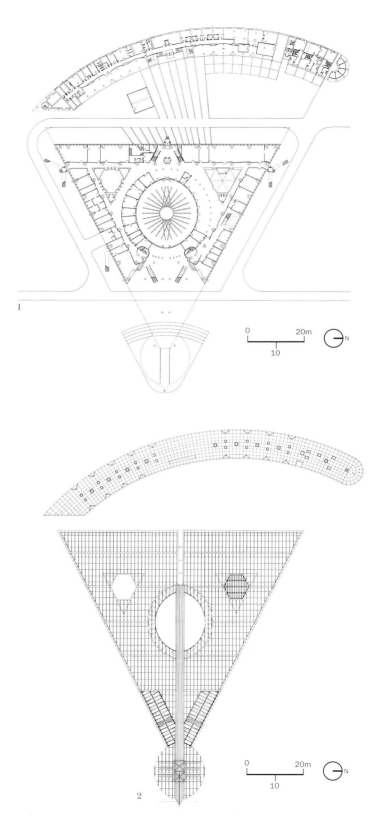

1 Ground floor plan
2 Roofing plan
3 Courtyard section
4 Flying wing
5–6 Aerial view

168

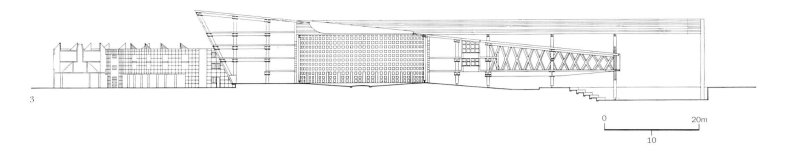

3

0   10   20m

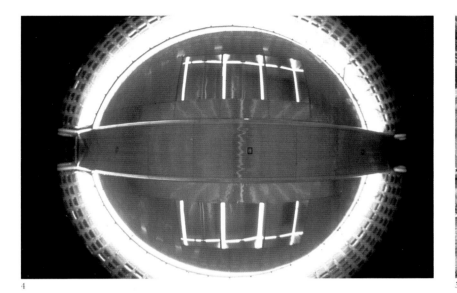

4

5

6

The High School of the Future applies the principle of contrasts: between fixedness and movement, between mass and lightness, between curved and straight lines, between the outside and the inside, between the present and the future.

7

8

7 Eastern accommodation frontage
8 Elliptical courtyard
9 The flying wing above the courtyard
10 Elliptical courtyard

9

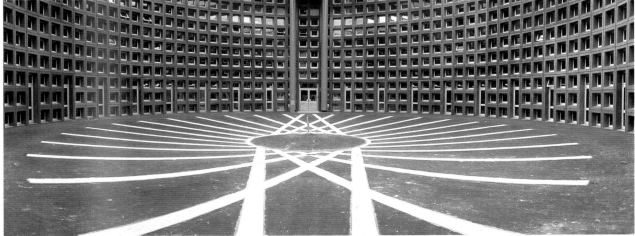

10

11

12

13

14

15

11 Passageway on the ground floor
12 View of bow
13 Traffic area
14 View of roof
15 Detail of accommodation frontage

16

17

174

16 The restaurant
17 Traffic area between classrooms
18 The northwest angle
19 Southern frontage

18

19

Apartment building in the Rue du Château-des-Rentiers

Design/Completion 1984/1986
Paris
Habitat Social Français
1,300 square metres

The first product of an approach aimed at using the residual blocks scattered around Paris. The building is on a small triangular plot in the 13th arrondissement. On this 150 square metre block, dominated by a blind wall over 30 metres in height, an 11-level landmark building comprising 25 apartments. A system of stilts clears the ground of any construction and the ground remains an open space.

The smallness of the land inverts the ratio between living space and facade surface. The facades become disproportionate and their function is radically changed. Thus, the great north wall comes to terms with this lack of proportion by integrating a gigantic map of the district, which lights up at night showing the bus and metro stations that have been marked out on the map. Inhabitable street furniture, this structure partakes in a more general interpretation of the city of which it merely wants to appear as a fragment.

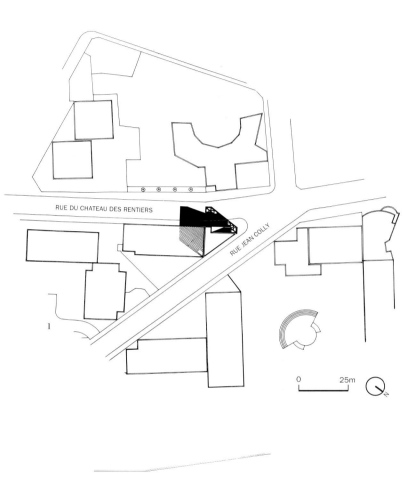

RUE DU CHATEAU DES RENTIERS

RUE JEAN COLLY

1

0   25m

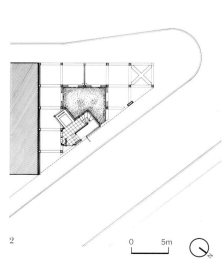

2

0   5m

3

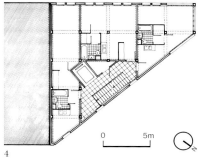

4

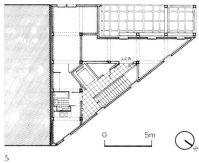

5

1 Block plan
2 Ground floor plan
3 Northern facade
4 Stock floor plan
5 Tenth floor plan

6 Detail of the public space on the ground floor
7 Public space on the ground floor
8 View of bow

6

7

8

Apartment building in the Rue du Château-des-Rentiers   179

9

10

11

12

13

14

9 Detail of southern frontage
10 Public space on the ground floor
11 Detail of bow
12 View from the west
13 Detail of northern frontage, seen by night
14 Northern frontage, seen by night

"Tête de la Défense"

Design 1983
Paris
Public Development Corporation of the Défense Quarter
150,000 square metres

The challenge was to build on the horizon. The horizon of one of the most universally known perspectives. The temptation to step aside was great, but the Défense has been built. The towers frame the profile of the Étoile Triumphal Arch and, in the centre, the void becomes artificial, a sign of powerlessness, of inability to build a landmark representing the architecture of this century.

The building idealises a horizon consisting of the sky, the light, the setting sun, a changing horizon, variable according to the weather, the distance, the conscience, the way of looking. A square, refined, abstract frame materialises the distant horizon. From the Carrousel and the Tuileries, the sky under the Triumphal Arch is woven at regular intervals. It is a cross-ruling of the landscape.

The horizon is being built. The horizon is variable. Thanks to the aluminium which reflects the colours and the ambient light, the geometry is itself permeated with the nuances of each instant, its intensity changes with the time of day, the back light and the clouds filtering the sky.

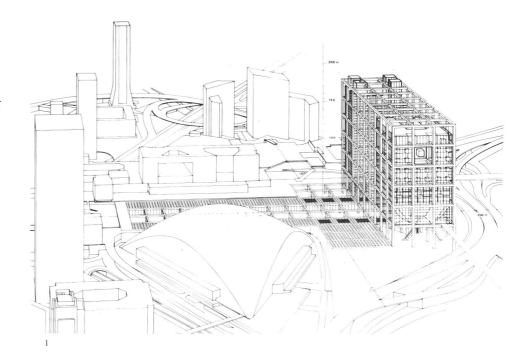

1

2

3

4

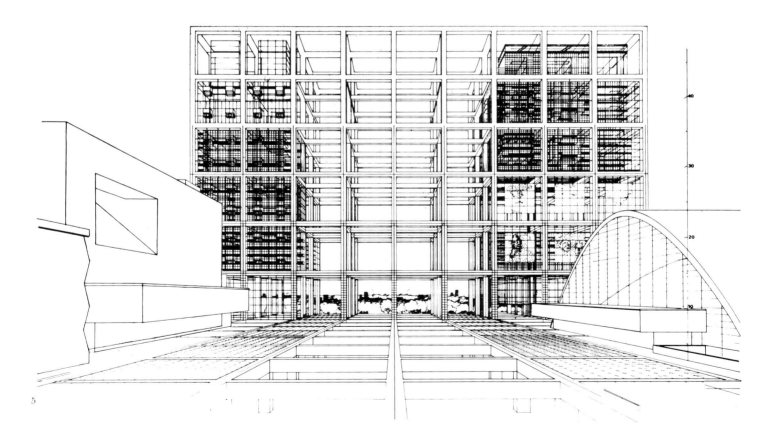

5

Kindergarten and primary school

Design/Completion 1982/1985
Paris
City of Paris
5,800 square metres

The kindergarten and primary school are located in an area characterised by buildings up to 17 storeys high sited along modernist lines.

It is an open school, highly visible from the pedestrian mall, the courtyards open onto this street and the interiority of this school is quite perceptible. The large proportions and profile—despite the low height of the school—of the side facing the courtyard, seen through a transparent portico, alongside the pedestrian mall, asserts a monumentality based on the extrapolation from building sets (Lego...).

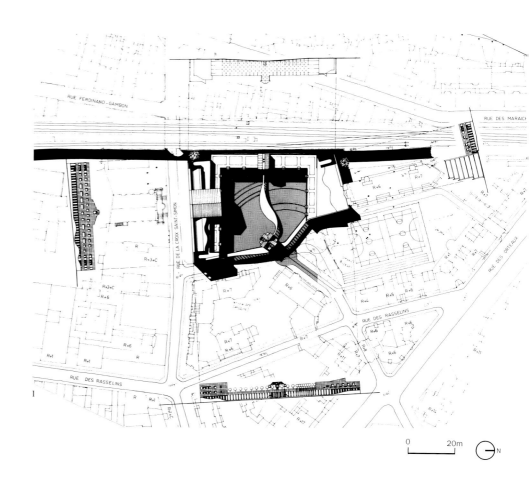

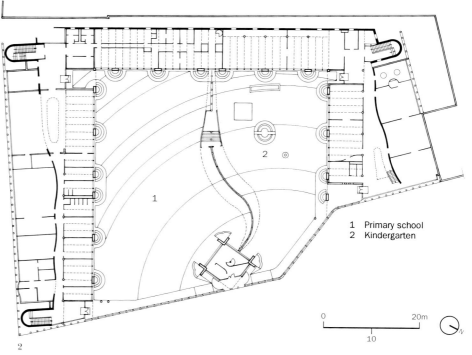

1 Primary school
2 Kindergarten

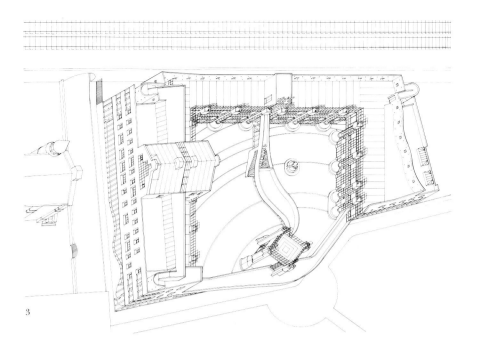

3

1 Location plan
2 Ground floor plan
3 Axonometry
4 Detail of the Rue de la Croix St-Simon frontage

4

5

The building follows the street alignment. It is contextual. It asserts the street all the more since it maintains and transposes the scale of the chapel situated across the road. Its profile is modern. The gymnasium, which crosses this building, looks out over the schoolyard. Nevertheless, the internal configuration of the school has its own logic and its own orthogonality. The joining of these two rigorous systems has permitted an unconstrained and aleatory treatment. The meeting of the two construction principles with its conflictual points happens to be the pupils' meeting point.

6

7

8

9

10

11

Apartment building in the Rue Domrémy

Design/Completion 1982/1984
Paris
Habitat Social Français
1,700 square metres

An extremely precise architecture, a windowed wall facing the street, designed on a grid system, without any shadows or external profiling.

The depth of the building is expressed by recessed gangways, of complex shapes, on which the shadows of the frame will assert the opposition of the very precise pre-facade facing the street and the internal masonry wall, coated and painted with a mixture of colours.

The treatment of shadows of the depth of the building is denoted by moulding on the facade. The transposition of features of the municipal school opposite asserts the will to retain the street. The roof becomes a glass roof and the upper part of the roof expresses the fracture of the building, as it may appear that the glass roof is capped by the upper part of the roof.

The project expresses the achievements of the city, of history, of the modern movement, while creating an excessive link between the alignments and neighbouring buildings.

1

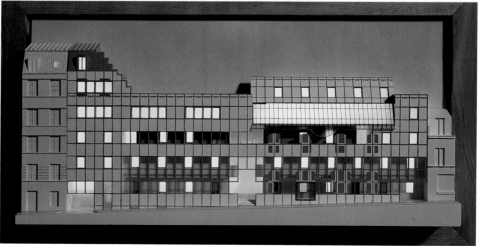

2

3

1   Rue Domrémy frontage
2   Sketch of street frontage, seen by night
3   Detail of the Rue Domrémy frontage

4

4 Detail of the courtyard wall
5 Space between railings and frontage
6 Detail of the Rue Domrémy frontage
7 Traffic area

5

6

Institute of the Arab World

Design/Completion 1981/1987
Paris
Institute of the Arab World
27,000 square metres

The head office of the Insitute of the Arab
World takes into account, in dialectical
terms, both aspects of the site: traditional
quarter and modern quarter, Arab culture
and Western culture, modernity and history,
inwardness and opening.

Its symbolism and modernity are based on
a present-day interpretation of the history of
these two civilisations. The land, situated at
the junction of two urban fabrics, one
traditional (continuous), the other more
modern (discontinuous) maintains a
dialogue with these two types of urban
planning.

The north side (facing the historical Paris),
the skin of the museum, symbolises the
relationship of the exhibits with the city,
hence the retranscription of the Île Saint-Louis
facade and surrounding Parisian landscape.
The south side, the skin of the library, is
based on traditional themes of the Arab
artistic geometry.

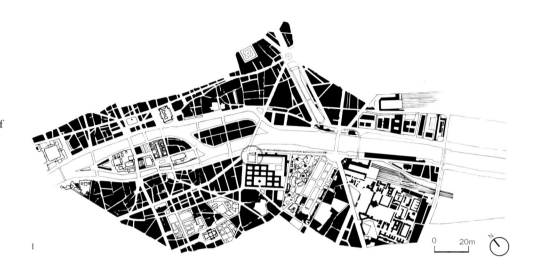

1

0   20m

2

1   Location plan
2   Southern frontage
3   Plan of level +17.40 (level R+6)
4   Building in its context

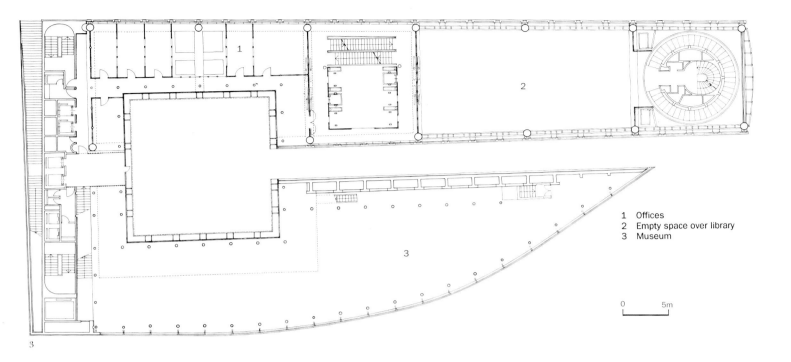

3

1 Offices
2 Empty space over library
3 Museum

0   5m

4

Eye protection is built into the windows by means of a variable frame based on the principle of the diaphragm. Photoelectric cells are used to modify the light according to the amount of sunshine. The diaphragms open and close depending on the external luminosity.

This project received the Équerre d'Argent award in 1988 and the Aga Khan Award in 1989.

5

6

5   Tip of building seen from the Ile Saint-Louis
6   Facade on the Seine, seen by night
7   Cross-section of patio and auditorium
8   Plan level 0.00 (level of ground floor and courtyard)

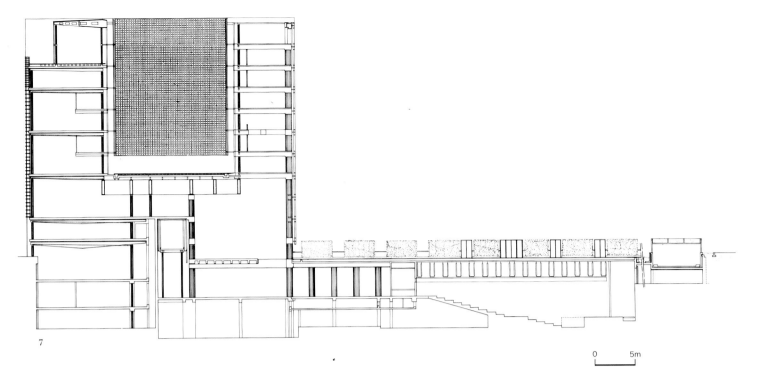

7

0   5m

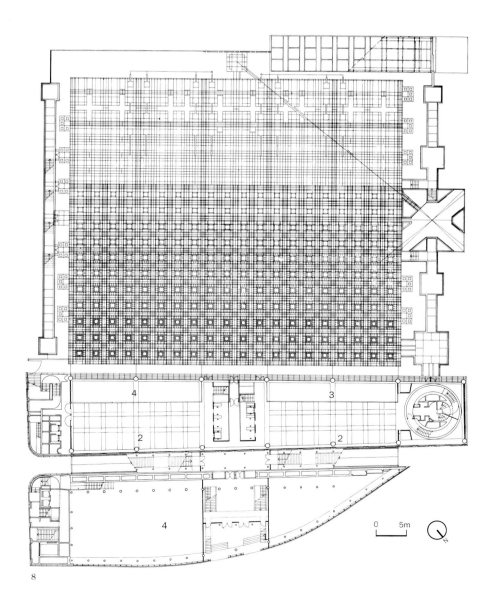

1 Hall
2 Reception hall
3 Empty space above the contemporary hall
4 Empty space above the hall
   of temporary exhibits

0   5m

8

9

10

11

9 Detail of the tower of books
10 Museum space
11 Detail on the museum's interior

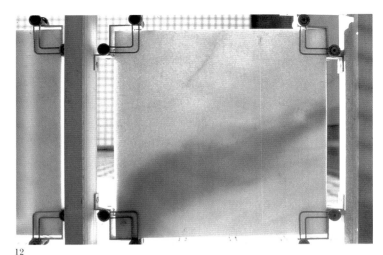

12

12 Detail of the patio frontage
13 Southern frontage—diaphram frontage with diaphrams open
14 Detail on the ceiling of the Hall of High Council

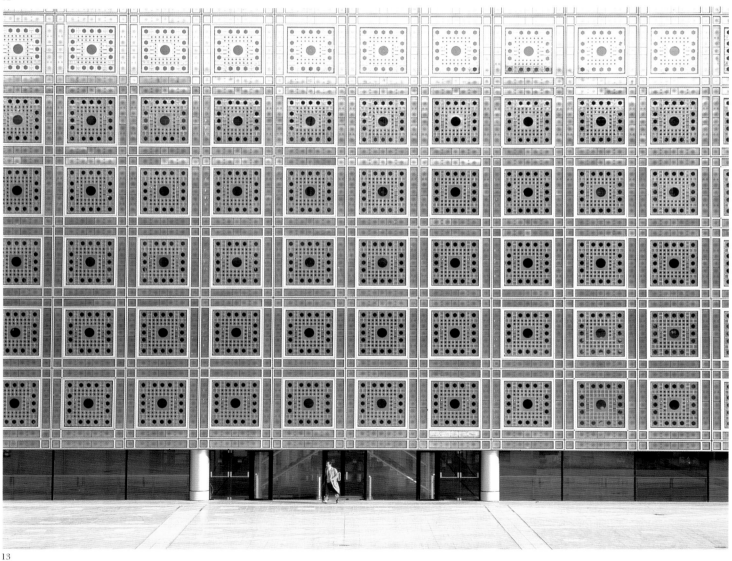

13

14

15 Main staircase
16 Southern frontage seen through the entrance way

Héraud residence

Design/Completion 1981/1983
Chasseneuil-du-Poitou
Mr and Mrs Héraud
210 square metres

Located at the confluence of two rivers, the project takes into account all the client's cultural achievements and amplifies them: the roof, the monumentality, the appearance, the theatre, the disproportion (the columns), the symmetry, the pediment, the preciosity, the conventional materials that have been used at cross-purposes.

The pediment, for example, at the client's express request, is made of aluminium tubing, situated in the axis of the house, but set at an angle in order to signify a desire for dissymmetry. Its meaning has been enhanced. The same goes for all the ingredients that make up the house. Postmodernism was the obligatory rite of passage to rediscover modernity.

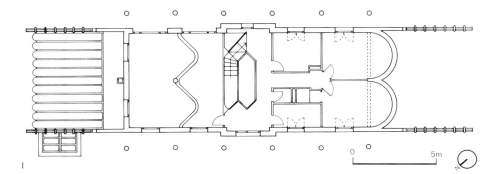

1

2

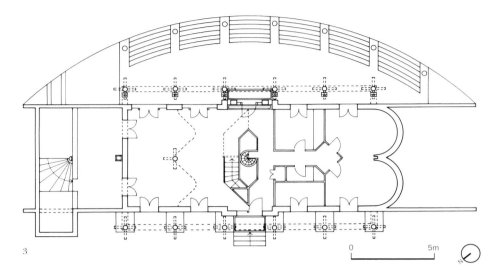

3

4

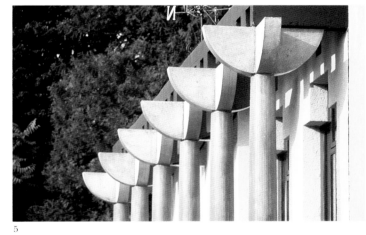

5

6

1   First floor plan
2   General view from the west
3   Ground floor plan
4   Detail of entrance, west frontage
5   Detail of the frontage
6   Detail of the east frontage

Renovation of façades on the Boulevard de Courcelles

Design/Completion 1981/1984
Paris
Public company for the rue de Monceau buildings

An architectural opportunity, this project involves creating a casing around the existing building. The contrast of the new profile takes on a strong and ambiguous meaning and recreates modernity.

The openings are in the same line as the existing ones. The empty spaces are crowned by enamelled sheet metal capitals creating a counter-column effect. The solid sections are made of bright, mass-coloured concrete, with accurate marking of shuttering panel holes and nail heads. The hollow columns are framed by a tile *modénature*.

Form and function are divorced. Columns do without posts. It does not have a material form. Its silhouette can be found in a hollow, in an opening. Implied reference, derision, and demonstration that no shape, no composition is beautiful *per se* and that an assemblage of ugliness, if it is meaningful, can be moving and beautiful.

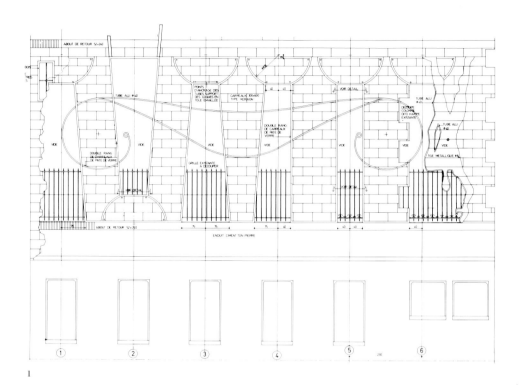

1

2

3

1   Boulevard de Courcelles frontage
2   Detail of the boulevard frontage
3   General view from the boulevard

Tihama cultural centre

Design 1981
Jeddah, Saudi Arabia
Tihama
30,000 square metres

The purpose of the Tihama cultural centre is to enable the progress of man in the Islamic tradition. The heterogeneous diversity of the elements making up the urban fabric of the city of Jeddah precludes the centre from being placed in a stylistic continuity of an architectural nature.

Despite this, points of reference have been selected, from daily experiences going back to the earliest arab antiquity, born of the desert: the organisation of a day in the Moslem life based on the Koran and the five laws, the fight against the heat and the harsh light, the free circulation of air and wind, the utilisation of coolness, shade, water, greenery in their relationship with the arid mineral.

1

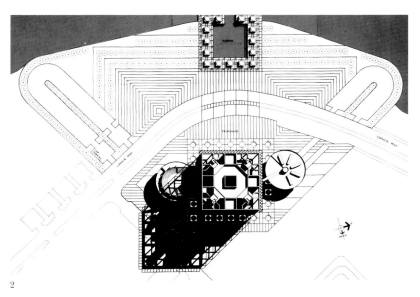

2

3

1   Interior elevation
2   Block plan
3   View of the model

Architectural agency

Design/Completion 1979/1980
Paris
1,000 square metres

In Paris, near the Bastille, a former locksmith
workshop, in a courtyard, only accessible
through a portico that crosses a bourgeois
building from end to end. The structure
has been kept intact. Only a few staircases,
a few balustrades, one or two partitions
have been added or removed. The site
retains its own memory and is perfectly suited
to its new role. It has become an office,
neither open, nor closed. An office with
a difference. Memory of the site, a slow
process that respects the rhythm and
movement of life itself through construction,
not destruction.

1

1–2   View of the central space
  3   View from a gangway

Convalescent home

Design/Completion 1972/1975
Clamart
Our Lady of the Sacred Heart Hermitage
3,400 square metres

Architecture Studio's first work, the
building is located at the top of a very
beautiful wooded plot of land, close to the
centre of town. It comprises 50 individual
rooms with a large number of internal and
external common areas, that are open to
convalescents. The influence of Louis
Kahn and Le Corbusier can be found in
this building.

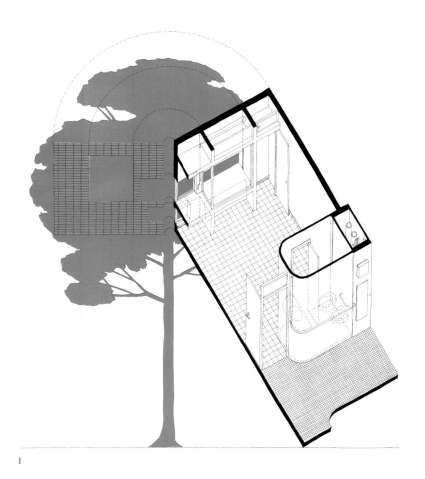

1

2

3

4

5

FIRM PROFILE

Biography

ARCHITECTURE STUDIO

R. Tisnado, M. Robain, A. Bretagnolle, R.-H. Arnaud, J.-F. Bonne, L.-M. Fischer

1973–1980

Founded in 1973, Architecture Studio today comprises six associates: Martin Robain, Rodo Tisnado, Jean-Francois Bonne, Alain Bretagnolle, René-Henri Arnaud, Laurent-Marc Fischer. Constituted along intellectual lines, the team had an open-door policy and grew bigger with the passage of time: Martin Robain since 1973, Jean-Francois Galmiche from 1974 to 1989, Rodo Tisnado since 1976, Francois-Xavier Désert from 1979 to 1985, Jean-Francois Bonne since 1979, Alain Bretagnolle and René-Henri Arnaud since 1989, and Laurent-Marc Fischer since 1993.

In 1980, they moved to the Rue Lacuée premises, near the Bastille district, to large open workshops dating from the late nineteenth century—a maze of bright, high and low-ceilinged rooms with a friendly and efficient ambience.

Co-founders of the "March 76" movement that wanted to establish a link between the decision-makers and the people, so that the latter were more closely involved in the development of their living environment.

Co-founders of the "Syndicat de l'architecture", an association that wanted to formulate demands in cultural, rather than professional, terms.

Their construction projects included a convalescent home at Clamart —characterised by the use of primary colours and the didactic authority of structure and form that was to remain their trademark even though it was gradually internalised and conceptualised—and the SAP apartments in Poitiers, an experimental construction with shared activity areas.

1981–1988

Construction of the Rue Domrémy apartments and the Rue Mouraud school—an explosion of colours, materials and lines. Architecture took on a new dimension and found a more playful expression. In the Rue du Château-des-Rentiers, on a small block, they built a landmark building that completed the angle of two streets and offered passers-by a fountain and a gigantic facade area map; a prototype building of a study called "Stimuli" on residual blocks in Paris; the Institute of the Arab World in Paris—built with the participation of Jean Nouvel, Gilbert Lezenes and Pierre Soria who shared the same premises at the time; the French Embassy in Muscat and the High School of the Future at Jaunay-Clan.

1989–1991

Many young architects of different nationalities joined Architecture Studio, eager to try an approach which they regarded as "topical, extremist and avant-garde". They noted that Architecture Studio steered clear of dogmas and schools of thought. At the agency, they discovered that the apparent fantasy of the projects—this humour of form and meaning, this plastic jubilation of materials that had won them over—was based on a rigorous discipline, a desire to be precise, and also the authority of the associates whose method guaranteed the productive operation of the group. This approach could be summed up by the axiom: collective demands are greater than the sum of individual demands.

Some of the major works of this period include: the Gennevilliers fire station, the National Judo Institute in Paris, the Our Lady of the Covenant Church in Paris, the business centre in Besançon, the Arènes High School in Toulouse. They won the international competition for the European Parliament in Strasbourg.

1991–1994

Construction of the Jules Verne High School at Cergy-le-Haut, the Forum des Arènes in Toulouse, the post office and mail sorting centre on the Boulevard de la Chapelle in Paris. They won the competition to build the École des Mines in Albi and the Law Courts in Caen. Work started on the construction of the European Parliament—a project symbolic of democracy.

Foundation in 1991 of D. Studio which meets the very specific requirements of interior architecture, stylistic design, graphic design and signage.

Foundation in 1993 of Architecture Studio Europe which concerns itself more with European projects.

Associates and Collaborators as of December 1994

Associates

Martin Robain
Rodo Tisnado
Jean-François Bonne
Alain Bretagnolle
René-Henri Arnaud
Laurent-Marc Fischer

Collaborators

Peter Allenbach
Virginie Anselme
Pierre Auffan
Jean-François Authier
Roueïda Ayache
Jane Bacon
Mohammad Badreddine
Neale Bairstow
Bertram Beissel von Gymnich
Enrico Benedetti
Rabah Bentoumi
Aurélie Berthet
Nilberto Gomez de Souza
Armelle Bolivard
Anne Bon
Sandrine Bonneville
Françoise Boucher
Daniel Chang
Tina Chee
Didier Colin
Dominique Cornaert
Patrick Cosmao
Philippe Coste
Claudis Cristea
Domitille Desjobert
Peter Duck
Elisabeth Dufourg
Antoine Durand
Sandrine Elice
Sanne Elkaer
Frigo
Lynn Fullerton
Nicolas Girard
Arnaud Goujon
Corinne Granger
Mathieu Guillaume
Ann Guillec
Carol Guinebert
Isabelle Gunasena
Christian Hofbauer
Eric Hugel
Danièle Josephine
David Kohn

Laurence Krupa
Catherine Lauvray
Martha Leblanc
Emmanuelle Le Chevallier
Jacques Ledu
Marc Lehmann
Chantal Lerolle
Pierre Lesbats
Youssef Mallat Lopez
Bruno Mary
Gian Maurizio
Anna Matrakidou-Foukas
Fabrice Messier
François Napoly
Frédéric Neau
Olivier Paurd
Oliver Perceval
Constantin Petcou
Olivier Petit
Sophie Petit
Laurent Pezin
Nathalie Pollet
Fernando Quintana
Pierre Reibel
Romain Reuther
Philippe Robles
Philippe Sardin
Jeff Schoffield
Cyril Simonot
Agnès Sole
Igor Strzok
Véronique Toutain
Augustin de Tugny
Matthew Viederman
Carole Vilet
Denis Walther
Jane Wrightson
Zaini Zainul
Stéphane Zamfirescu

Chronological List of Buildings and Projects

* Indicates work featured in this book
(See Selected and Current Works)

1994

Technical and Professional
University Institute
  Magdeburg, Germany
  Client: City of Magdeburg, Ministry of Finance (Germany)
  Architects: Architecture Studio (M. Robain, R. Tisnado, J.-F. Bonne,
  A. Bretagnolle, R.-H. Arnaud, L.-M. Fischer)
  Assistants: T. Marco, C. Petcou
  Engineering: Trouvin Ingénierie, H.L. Technik
  Surface: 18,000 square metres
  Competition awarded

Greater Noumea High School
  Dumbea, New Caledonia
  Client: Ministry of National Education
  Architects: Architecture Studio (M. Robain, R. Tisnado, J.-F. Bonne,
  A. Bretagnolle, R.-H. Arnaud, L.-M. Fischer)
  Assistants: Frigo, V. Anselme, J.-F. Authier
  Engineering: O.T.H. International
  Surface: 16,700 square metres
  Competition

New Upper Corsica prefecture building
  Bastia, Corsica
  Client: Ministry of the Interior and Country Planning, Prefecture of Upper Corsica
  Architects: Architecture Studio (M. Robain, R. Tisnado, J.-F. Bonne,
  A. Bretagnolle, R.-H. Arnaud, L.-M. Fischer)
  Assistants: M. Lehmann, P. Auffan, N. Pollet, P. Duck
  Engineering: Serete Régions
  Consultant: P. Niez (landscape)
  Surface: 8,000 square metres
  Competition

Cannes-la-Bocca hospital complex [1]
  Cannes
  Architects: Architecture Studio (M. Robain, R. Tisnado, J.-F. Bonne, A. Bretagnolle,
  R.-H. Arnaud, L.-M. Fischer)
  Assistants: C. Petcou, J.-F. Authier, M. Badreddine, A. Bon, V. Anselme, J. Rathle,
  C. Simonot, Frigo, D. Kohn
  Engineering: Serete Régions
  Surface: 60,000 square metres
  Competition, award winning entry
  Delivery: 2,000

1

Georges Brassens High School
  Villepinte
  Client: Île-de-France Regional Council
  Architects: Architecture Studio (M. Robain, R. Tisnado, J.-F. Bonne,
  A. Bretagnolle, R.-H. Arnaud, L.-M. Fischer)
  Assistants: O. Petit, C. Simonot
  Engineering: Technip Seri Construction
  Consultant: P. Niez (landscape)
  General contractor: S.A.E.P.
  Surface: 8,000 square metres
  Competition

Chronological List of Buildings and Projects

Training and Research University [(2)]
University Campus II, Caen
Client: Upper Normandy Region
Architects: Architecture Studio (M. Robain, R. Tisnado, J.-F. Bonne,
A. Bretagnolle, R.-H. Arnaud, L.-M. Fischer)
Assistants: M. Lehmann, P. Auffan
Engineering: Serete Régions
Surface: 16,000 square metres
Competition

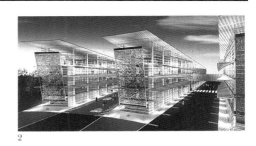
2

*Super Stadium for the 1998
World Soccer Cup
Paris-Saint-Denis
Client: Interministerial delegation to the 1998 World Soccer Cup
Architects: Architecture Studio (M. Robain, R. Tisnado, J.-F. Bonne,
A. Bretagnolle, R.-H. Arnaud, L.-M. Fischer) and Valode & Pistre and associates
Assistants: M. Lehmann, O. Petit
Consultants: Ove Arup (structure), Casso & Cie (safety), Desvignes & Dalnoky (landscape)
Contractors: Dumez, Bouygues, S.G.E.
Modular 80,000-seat stadium
International competition

*Scenography for the "Press review:
A report on information clearing-houses" exhibition
Arsenal Pavilion, Paris
Client: City of Paris, Arsenal Pavilion
Architects: Architecture Studio (M. Robain, R. Tisnado, J.-F. Bonne,
A. Bretagnolle, R.-H. Arnaud, L.-M. Fischer)
Assistants: A. de Tugny, A. Heaume
Consultants: Futur Vision-Innovision (multimedia), Ikor (composite materials)
Delivery: 1994

Our Lady of Whitsun Church [(3)]
Paris-La Défense
Client: Nanterre Diocesan Association, Les Chantiers du Cardinal.
Architects: Architecture Studio (M. Robain, R. Tisnado, J.-F. Bonne,
A. Bretagnolle, R.-H. Arnaud, L.-M. Fischer)
Assistants: F. Neau, J. Davis, E, Benedetti
Advisor: S. Landes
Consultants: Ikor (composite materials, structure), A.T.E.C. (economy),
E. Vivié (acoustics)
Surface: 1,500 square metres
Competition

3

Retirement home with medical care
Campagne-les-Hesdin
Client: Montreuil-sur-Mer General Hospital
Architects: Architecture Studio (M. Robain, R. Tisnado, J.-F. Bonne,
A. Bretagnolle, R.-H. Arnaud, L.-M. Fischer)
Competition

Scenography for the play *The Winter's Tale* [(4)]
Paris
Client: Théâtre du Fresne
Architects: Architecture Studio (M. Robain, R. Tisnado, J.-F. Bonne,
A. Bretagnolle, R.-H. Arnaud, L.-M. Fischer)
Assistant: O. Tossan
Delivery: 1994

4

*Church
Rome, Italy
Client: Vicariate of Rome
Architects: Architecture Studio (M. Robain, R. Tisnado, J.-F. Bonne,
A. Bretagnolle, R.-H. Arnaud, L.-M. Fischer)
Assistant: E. Benedetti
Associated architect: P. Fioravanti
Surface: 1,500 square metres
International competition, project accepted

*Rebuilding of souks
    Beirut, Lebanon
    Client: Solidere
    Architects: Architecture Studio (M. Robain, R. Tisnado, J.-F. Bonne,
    A. Bretagnolle, R.-H. Arnaud, L.-M. Fischer)
    Assistants: E. Benedetti, J.-M. Bonfils, J. Davis, M. Van Eijs, M. Viederman
    Associated architect: M. Bonfils
    Surface: 135,000 square metres
    International competition

1993

*Exhibition ground
    Paris-Nord Villepinte
    Client: Paris-Nord Villepinte Exhibition Ground Operating company,
    Paris Chamber of Commerce and Industry
    Architects: Architecture Studio (M. Robain, R. Tisnado, J.-F. Bonne, A. Bretagnolle,
    R.-H. Arnaud, L.-M. Fischer), Valode & Pistre and associates and Avant-Travaux Architectes
    Assistants: I. Gunasena, P. Dubus, B. Beissel von Gymnich, G. Maurizio
    Surface: 500,000 square metres
    International competition by invitation, two award-winning projects:
    Architecture Studio, Avant-Travaux Architectes and Valode & Pistre and associates, then
    development of a single project by Architecture Studio, Valode & Pistre and associates,
    and Avant-Travaux Architectes

*FIMAT office development
    Hôtel de Bony 32, rue de Trévise—75009 Paris
    Client: FIMAT
    Architects: Architecture Studio (M. Robain, R. Tisnado, J.-F. Bonne,
    A. Bretagnolle, R.-H. Arnaud, L.-M. Fischer), D. Studio (S. Petit, A. de Tugny)
    Assistants: L. Massaloux, V. Béranger
    Engineering: Noble Ingénierie
    Surface: 600 square metres
    Competition by invitation, award-winning project
    Delivery: 1994

Rehabilitation of an apartment building
    169, rue Pelleport—75020 Paris
    Client: O.P.A.C., of Paris
    Architects: Architecture Studio (M. Robain, R. Tisnado, J.-F. Bonne,
    A. Bretagnolle, R.-H. Arnaud, L.-M. Fischer)
    Assistants: N. Girard, N. Pollet
    Engineering: C.O.T.E.C.
    Competition by invitation, award-winning project
    Delivery scheduled for 1995

Activity centre (5)
    Zac Berges de Seine—92110 Clichy
    Client: Entreprise Bechet
    Client nominee: Les Bâtisseurs de France
    Developer: Société d'économie mixte Clichy Expansion
    Architects: Architecture Studio (M. Robain, R. Tisnado, J.-F. Bonne,
    A. Bretagnolle, R.-H. Arnaud, L.-M. Fischer)
    Assistant: I. Gunasena
    Engineering: Serete
    Surface: 34,000 square metres
    Delivery scheduled for 1995

5

**Rehabilitation of a general
and vocational high school**
    Vitry-le-Francois
    Client: Champagne Ardennes Region
    Architects: Architecture Studio (M. Robain, R. Tisnado, J.-F. Bonne,
    A. Bretagnolle, R.-H. Arnaud, L.-M. Fischer) and Avant Travaux Architectes
    Surface: 10,000 square metres
    Competition

Chronological List of Buildings and Projects

Development of the Spreeinsel district
Berlin, Germany
Client: City of Berlin
Architects: Architecture Studio (M. Robain, R. Tisnado, J.-F. Bonne,
A. Bretagnolle, R.-H. Arnaud, L.-M. Fischer)
Assistant: G. Kalhofer
International ideas competition

School of Engineering and Mechanics Institute [6]
Saint-Étienne-du-Rouvray
Client: Ministry of Culture and National Education,
Rouen Education Authority
Architects: Architecture Studio (M. Robain, R. Tisnado, J.-F. Bonne,
A. Bretagnolle, R.-H. Arnaud)
Assistants: N. Girard, P. Bona, J.-F. Authier
Engineers: Serete Régions
Surface: 15,000 square metres
Competition

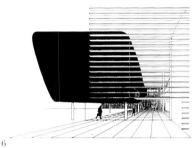

6

Extension of the Jean Monnet University [7]
2, rue Tréfilerie—42023 Saint-Étienne
Client: City of Saint-Étienne
Architects: Architecture Studio (M. Robain, R. Tisnado, J.-F. Bonne,
A. Bretagnolle, R.-H. Arnaud)
Assistants: R. Reuther, J. Bacon, J. Van der Goot
Associated architects: Groupe Cimaise
Builder: Lantermoz
Contractor: L'Européenne d'Entreprise
Engineering: J. & P. Deville (structure), Gepral (fluids)
Consultant: Cyprium (economy)
Surface: 3,500 square metres
Competition, award-winning project
Delivery scheduled for 1995

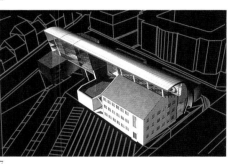

7

*Law Courts (Palais de Justice)
Zac Gardin, Place Gambetta—14000 Caen
Client: Ministry of Justice, D.G.P.P.E.
Architects: Architecture Studio (M. Robain, R. Tisnado, J.-F. Bonne,
A. Bretagnolle, R.-H. Arnaud)
Assistants: P. Sardin, P. Auffan, J. Bacon
Engineers: Oger International
Consultants: Ikor (composite materials), Les éclairagistes associés (lighting),
E. Vivié (acoustics), D. Studio (interior design)
Surface: 9,500 square metres
Competition, award-winning project
Delivery scheduled for 1996

Public Revenue Office
data processing department
Limoges
Client: Ministry of the Economy, Finance and the Budget
Architects: Architecture Studio (M. Robain, R. Tisnado, J.-F. Bonne,
A. Bretagnolle, R.-H. Arnaud)
Assistant: G. Maurizio
Engineers: S.A.2.I.
Contractor: Socae-Copreco
Surface: 6,800 square metres
Competition

Louis Pasteur University
Institute of Technology [8]
Schiltigheim
Client: Ministry of Culture and National Education,
Strasbourg Education Authority
Architects: Architecture Studio (M. Robain, R. Tisnado, J.-F. Bonne,
A. Bretagnolle, R.-H. Arnaud)
Assistants: S. Rotbard, J.-P. Giraud
Associated architect: G. Valente
Engineers: O.T.E. Ingénierie
Surface: 7,000 square metres
Competition

8

Development of city centre
Saint-Lô
Client: Saint-Lô City Council
Architects: Architecture Studio (M. Robain, R. Tisnado, J.-F. Bonne,
A. Bretagnolle, R.-H. Arnaud)
Assistant: L.-M. Fischer
Consultant: A. de Tugny (scenography, interior design), S. Antonin
(programming), B.-H. Vayssière (town planning)
Competition

Chevalley baths [9]
Aix-les-Bains
Client: Syndicat Mixte des Thermes Nationaux d'Aix-les-Bains, Société
d'Aménagement de la Savoie
Architects: Architecture Studio (M. Robain, R. Tisnado, J.-F. Bonne,
A. Bretagnolle, R.-H. Arnaud)
Assistants: L.-M. Fischer, J. Davis, N. Mercé Laval, G. Maurizio, S. Rotbard
Engineering: Technip Seri Construction
Surface: 15,000 square metres
Competition

9

Departmental Museum of Natural History
Rouen
Client: Seine Maritime Department
Architects: Architecture Studio (M. Robain, R. Tisnado, J.-F. Bonne,
A. Bretagnolle, R.-H. Arnaud)
Assistants: S. Eloire, J. Davis
Engineers: Sogelerg
Consultants: Scène (scenography), Casso & Cie (safety)
Surface: 9,000 square metres
Competition

Montbéliard Urban
District headquarters [10]
Montbéliard
Client: Montbéliard Urban District
Architects: Architecture Studio (M. Robain, R. Tisnado, J.-F. Bonne,
A. Bretagnolle, R.-H. Arnaud)
Assistant: R. Reuther
Engineers: G.I.A.
Surface: 6,000 square metres
Competition

10

1992

Raising of a house
13, rue Robert Blache —75010 Paris
Client: S.F.P.M.
Architects: Architecture Studio (M. Robain, R. Tisnado, J.-F. Bonne,
A. Bretagnolle, R.-H. Arnaud) D. Studio (S. Petit, A. de Tugny)
Assistant: M. Van Eys
Surface: 125 square metres
Delivery: 1996

Chronological List of Buildings and Projects

***Libraries and completion
of Jussieu Campus project**
  Paris
  Client: Ministry of Culture and National Education
  Architects: Architecture Studio (M. Robain, R. Tisnado, J.-F. Bonne,
  A. Bretagnolle, R.-H. Arnaud)
  Assistants: J. Davis, S. Eloire
  Engineers: Séchaud & Bossuyt
  Surface: 50,000 square metres
  International competition by invitation

11

Maurice Genevoix High School [11]
  Montrouge
  Client: Hauts-de-Seine General Council, S.E.M. 92
  Architects: Architecture Studio (M. Robain, R. Tisnado, J.-F. Bonne,
  A. Bretagnolle, R.-H. Arnaud)
  Assistants: P. Steller, V. Dubois, N. Mecattaf, Y. Bouchard
  Engineers: Séchaud & Bossuyt
  Surface: 13,000 square metres
  Competition

12

C.N.R.A. Nord extension [12]
  Athis-Mons
  Client: Ministry of Road and Building Infrastructure, Housing and Transport
  Architects: Architecture Studio (M. Robain, R. Tisnado, J.-F. Bonne,
  A. Bretagnolle, R.-H. Arnaud)
  Engineers: Séchaud & Bossuyt
  Surface: 8,500 square metres
  Competition

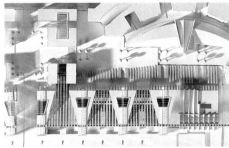
13

Air France head office [13]
  Roissy
  Client: Air France
  Architects: Architecture Studio (M. Robain, R. Tisnado, J.-F. Bonne,
  A. Bretagnolle, R.-H. Arnaud)
  Surface: 35,000 square metres
  Competition

*Development of the Place de Francfort
  Lyon Part Dieu
  Client: Rhône and Lyons District Road and Building Infrastructure Corporation
  Architects: Architecture Studio (M. Robain, R. Tisnado, J.-F. Bonne,
  A. Bretagnolle, R.-H. Arnaud)
  Assistants: F. Lebard, J. Njoo
  Engineers: Séchaud & Bossuyt
  Surface: 85,000 square metres
  International competition by invitation

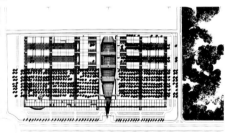
14

**National Institute of Applied Science
and Technology** [14]
  Tunis, Tunisia
  Client: Tunis Ministry of Education and Science
  Architects: Architecture Studio (M. Robain, R. Tisnado, J.-F. Bonne,
  A. Bretagnolle, R.-H. Arnaud)
  Associated architects: K. Mankai, S. Kraeim
  Surface: 28,000 square metres
  International competition

**Centre for Economic
and Financial Archives**
  Savigny-le-Temple
  Client: Ministry of the Economy, Finance and the Budget
  Architects: Architecture Studio (M. Robain, R. Tisnado, J.-F. Bonne,
  A. Bretagnolle, R.-H. Arnaud)
  Engineers: Sodeteg
  Surface: 10,000 square metres
  Competition

*City of Paris School of Fine Arts
  Paris
  Client: City of Paris
  Architects: Architecture Studio (M. Robain, R. Tisnado, J.-F. Bonne,
  A. Bretagnolle, R.-H. Arnaud)
  Assistants: J. Davis, N. Mecattaf
  Engineering: Séchaud & Bossuyt
  Surface: 18,000 square metres
  Competition

*Forum des Arènes
  4, place Émile Mâle—31024 Toulouse
  Client: M.T. Développement, S.C.E.T., C.I.F. Immo, S.A. H.L.M. les Chalets,
  S.C.I.C. A.M.O., Le Nouveau Logis Méridional
  Architects: Architecture Studio (M. Robain, R. Tisnado, J.-F. Bonne,
  A. Bretagnolle, R.-H. Arnaud)
  Assistants: M. Lehmann, J. Bacon
  Engineers: O.T.H. Sud-Ouest
  Surface: 35,000 square metres
  Delivery: 1994

Air Navigation
Technical Services [15]
  Toulouse
  Client: Ministry of Road and Building Infrastructure, Housing and Transport,
  Haute-Garonne Department Directorate of Road and Building Infrastructure
  Architects: Architecture Studio (M. Robain, R. Tisnado, J.-F. Bonne,
  A. Bretagnolle, R.-H. Arnaud)
  Assistant: V. Dubois
  Engineering: Sechaud & Bossuyt, B.E.F.S.
  Surface: 34,000 square metres
  Competition

15

*Albi-Carmaux École des Mines
  Jarlard site—81000 Albi
  Client: Ministry of Industry and Foreign Trade, Tarn Department Directorate of
  Road and Building Infrastructure
  Architects: Architecture Studio (M. Robain, R. Tisnado, J.-F. Bonne,
  A. Bretagnolle, R.-H. Arnaud)
  Assistants: L. Pezin, G. Maurizio
  Associated architect: G. Onesta
  Engineers: Sogelerg Sogreah
  Contractor: Les Travaux du Midi
  Surface: 35,000 square metres
  Competition, award-winning project
  Delivery scheduled for 1995

1991

*Jules Verne High School
  1, rue de la Marnière—95800 Cergy-le-Haut
  Client: Île-de-France Regional Council
  Client's assistant: Patrimoine Ingénierie S.A.
  Architects: Architecture Studio (M. Robain, R. Tisnado, J.-F. Bonne,
  A. Bretagnolle, R.-H. Arnaud, L.-M. Fischer)
  Assistants: S. Starkin, J. Bacon, A. Guillec, E. Hugel, F. Messier
  Engineers: Sofresid Bâtiment
  General contractor: Razel Bâtiment
  Sculpture: P. Kowalski
  Surface: 16,600 square metres
  Design-Building competition, award-winning project
  Delivery: 1993

*European Parliament
Quai Winterer—67000 Strasbourg
Client: Société d'Exploitation de la Région Strasbourgeoise
Architects: Architecture Studio (M. Robain, R. Tisnado, J.-F. Bonne,
A. Bretagnolle, R.-H. Arnaud)
Assistants: P. Allenbach, N. Bairstow, E. Benedetti, R. Bentoumi, T. Chee,
D. Cornaert, P. Cosmao, P. Coste, C. Cristea, E. Dufourg, A. Durand, S. Elkaer,
L. Fullerton, A. Goujon, L. Krupa, C. Lauvray, M. Leblanc, E. Le Chevallier,
P. Lesbats, A. Matrakidou-Foukas, F. Messier, F. Napoly, F. Neau, F. Quintana,
J. Schoffield, I. Strzok, D. Walther, M. Viederman, Z. Zainul
Associated architect: G. Valente
Engineering: Sogelerg, G.I.L. (O.T.E. ingénierie, Serue, E.T.F.)
Consultants: Desvignes & Dalnoky (landscape), Avant Travaux Architectes,
D. Studio (furniture), Arwytec (kitchen), A.V.L.S. (acoustics), C.E.E.F. (facades),
L'Observatoire 1 (lighting), C.O.M.E.N.T. (audiovisual), Casso & Cie (safety)
Surface: 180,000 square metres
International competition, award-winning project
Delivery scheduled for 1997

Office building
Versailles
Client: A.F.T.R.P., Cogedim Aménagement
Architects: Architecture Studio (M. Robain, R. Tisnado, J.-F. Bonne,
A. Bretagnolle, R.-H. Arnaud)
Surface: 25,000 square metres
Competition

Durzy general and technological
high school [16]
Montargis
Client: Centre Region
Architects: Architecture Studio (M. Robain, R. Tisnado, J.-F. Bonne,
A. Bretagnolle, R.-H. Arnaud)
Assistants: D. Tomalevski, T. Chan, S. Starkin, A. Guillec, J. Bacon
Engineers: O.T.H. Bâtiment
Surface: 32,000 square metres
Competition

16

Development of the Place Chalon [17]
Paris
Client: S.E.M.E.A.E.S.T.
Architects: Architecture Studio (M. Robain, R. Tisnado, J.-F. Bonne,
A. Bretagnolle, R.-H. Arnaud)
Surface: 60,000 square metres
Competition

Rotrou High School
Dreux
Client: Centre Region Regional Council
Architects: Architecture Studio (M. Robain, R. Tisnado, J.-F. Bonne,
A. Bretagnolle, R.-H. Arnaud)
Delivery: 1993

17

1990

Old people's home [18]
Rue de l'Orillon—75011 Paris
Client: Le Logement Francais
Architects: Architecture Studio (M. Robain, R. Tisnado, J.-F. Bonne,
A. Bretagnolle, R.-H. Arnaud, L.-M. Fischer)
Assistant: J. Davis, C. Simonot
Engineering: C.E.E.F. (facades), Choulet (fluids),
Scyna 4 (structure)
Consultant: D. Lucigny (economy)
Surface: 8,000 square metres
Delivery scheduled for 1996

18

*University restaurant
   10, place des Nations—59140 Dunkirk
   Client: Lille Education Authority, C.R.O.U.S.
   Architects: Architecture Studio (M. Robain, R. Tisnado, J.-F. Bonne,
   A. Bretagnolle, R.-H. Arnaud)
   Associated architects: Pixel (Verbauwen & Pouille)
   Engineers: O.T.H. Nord-Ouest
   Surface: 1,500 square metres
   Delivery: 1993

University technocity [19]
   Illkirch
   Client: Alsace Region, Strasbourg Urban Community
   Architects: Architecture Studio (M. Robain, R. Tisnado, J.-F. Bonne,
   A. Bretagnolle, R.-H. Arnaud)
   Assistants: M.-H. Maurette, X. Lauzeral
   Engineers: O.T.H.
   Surface: 25,000 square metres
   Competition

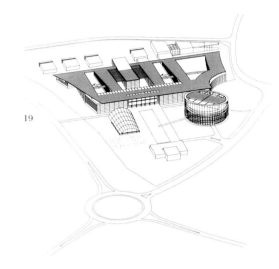

*Apartment building and
Jeanine Manuel Bilingual Active School
   9, 11,15, rue Edgar Faure—75015 Paris
   Developer: S.E.M.E.A. XV
   Client: S.A.G.I.
   Architects: Architecture Studio (M. Robain, R. Tisnado, J.-F. Bonne,
   A. Bretagnolle, R.-H. Arnaud)
   Assistants: R. Reuther, C. Gautié, F. Messier
   Engineers: B.E.C.T.
   Contractor: Guerra Tarcy
   Surface: 9,000 square metres
   Delivery: 1994

Urban project [20]
   Amiens
   Client: City of Amiens
   Architects: Architecture Studio (M. Robain, R. Tisnado, J.-F. Bonne,
   A. Bretagnolle, R.-H. Arnaud)
   Assistants: H. Wollensak, D. Lesbegueris, F. Vincendon, F. Rosadini
   Consultants: B.-H. Vayssière (town planning)
   Proposed urban development

*Renault Technology Centre
   Guyancourt
   Client: Régie Renault
   Architects: Architecture Studio (M. Robain, R. Tisnado, J.-F. Bonne,
   A. Bretagnolle, R.-H. Arnaud)
   Assistants: M. Gautrand, J.-P. Kerdoncuff, C. Gautié, T. Chan, R. Ayache
   Consultants: B.-H. Vayssière (town planning), M. Desvignes (landscape),
   M. Sardou (aerodynamics), T. Lacoste (image)
   Surface: 550,000 square metres
   Competition by invitation

* "Marché de l'Europe" business centre
   Îlot Treilhard, Paris
   Client: Groupe Pierre 1er
   Architects: Architecture Studio (M. Robain, R. Tisnado, J.-F. Bonne,
   A. Bretagnolle, R.-H. Arnaud)
   Assistants: H. Wollensak, J. Davis, M. Gautrand
   Engineers: Arcoba, Coteba
   Surface: 25,000 square metres
   Competition by invitation, award-winning project
   Project dropped

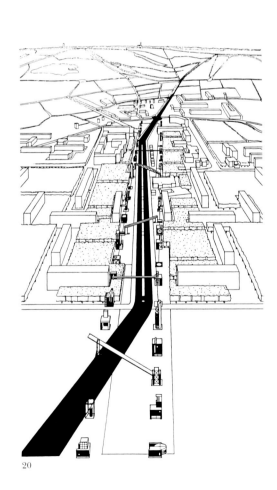

Chronological List of Buildings and Projects

Euroteleport office building [21]
 Roubaix
 Client: S.A.R.I.
 Architects: Architecture Studio (M. Robain, R. Tisnado, J.-F. Bonne,
 A. Bretagnolle, R.-H. Arnaud)
 Assistants: F. Magendie, C. Funk, J. Boissonade
 Engineers: Cotrasec
 Surface: 2,500 square metres
 Delivery: 1991

21

Rehabilitation of a university residence [22]
 Massy
 Client: S.C.I.C.
 Architects: Architecture Studio (M. Robain, R. Tisnado, J.-F. Bonne,
 A. Bretagnolle, R.-H. Arnaud)
 Assistants: A. Guillec, N. Mecattaf
 Engineers: Serequip
 Project dropped

22

Rue Wilhem apartment building [23]
 Paris
 Client: S.G.I.M. for the Health and Welfare Services
 Architects: Architecture Studio (M. Robain, R. Tisnado, J.-F. Bonne,
 A. Bretagnolle, R.-H. Arnaud)
 Assistants: R. Ayache, J.-P. Kerdoncuff
 Surface: 3,600 square metres

23

Citadel University extension
 Quai Freycinet—59140 Dunkirk
 Client: Dunkirk Urban Community
 Architects: Architecture Studio (M. Robain, R. Tisnado, J.-F. Bonne,
 A. Bretagnolle, R.-H. Arnaud)
 Assistants: R. Reuther, J. Bacon, H. Wollensak, G. Eustache
 Engineers: Serete Nord
 Contractor: S.T.T.-E.P.S.-Dumez
 Surface: 3,600 square metres
 Delivery: 1995

*Doctor's surgery
 4, rue Pasteur—77400 Lagny-sur-Marne
 Client: F.-X. Sallée
 Architects: Architecture Studio (M. Robain, R. Tisnado, J.-F. Bonne,
 A. Bretagnolle, R.-H. Arnaud) D. Studio (S. Petit)
 Assistant: P. Lepinay
 Consultant: D. Studio (planning)
 Surface: 120 square metres
 Delivery: 1991

Center Ain Department [24]
 Bourg-en-Bresse
 Client: City of Bourg-en-Bresse, Ain Department
 Architects: Architecture Studio (M. Robain, R. Tisnado, J.-F. Bonne,
 A. Bretagnolle, R.-H. Arnaud)
 Assistants: P. Lepinay, S. Planchez
 Engineers: Technip Seri Construction
 Surface: 7,000 square metres
 Competition

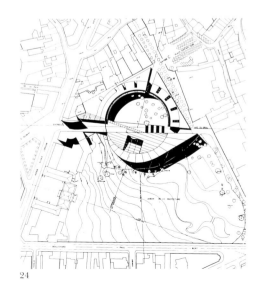

Convention centre
 Belfort
 Client: City of Belfort
 Architects: Architecture Studio (M. Robain, R. Tisnado, J.-F. Bonne,
 A. Bretagnolle, R.-H. Arnaud)
 Assistants: J.-P. Kerdoncuff, M.-H. Maurette
 Engineering: Acora, A.P.I.A.
 Surface: 6,000 square metres
 Competition

24

Rehabilitation of a building in the Rue Nationale
Paris
Client: City of Paris
Architects: Architecture Studio (M. Robain, R. Tisnado, J.-F. Bonne,
A. Bretagnolle, R.-H. Arnaud)
Assistant: F. Magendie
Competition

Redevelopment of city centre
Villeneuve d'Ascq
Client: City of Villeneuve d'Ascq
Architects: Architecture Studio (M. Robain, R. Tisnado, J.-F. Bonne,
A. Bretagnolle, R.-H. Arnaud)
Assistants: M.-H. Maurette, J. Davis
Engineers: S.C.E.T.
Consultant: B.-H. Vayssière (town planning)
Competition

Apartment building [25]
11, rue Cauchy—75015 Paris
Client: S.A.G.I.
Developer: S.E.M.E.A. XV
Architects: Architecture Studio (M. Robain, R. Tisnado, J.-F. Bonne,
J.-F. Galmiche, A. Bretagnolle, R.-H. Arnaud)
Assistants: C. Vilet, E. Hugel, D. Lesbegueris, S. Planchez, F. Messier, F. Rabiet
Engineers: B.E.C.T.
Contractor: Bouygues
Delivery scheduled for 1997

25

1989

French Institute of Advanced Mechanics [26]
Clermont-Ferrand
Client: Clermont-Ferrand Education Authority
Architects: Architecture Studio (M. Robain, R. Tisnado, J.-F. Bonne,
J.-F. Galmiche, A. Bretagnolle, R.-H. Arnaud)
Assistants: P. Dutertre, R. Ayache
Engineers: B.E.F.S.–T.E.C.
Surface: 12,500 square metres
Competition

*Cayenne–Rochambeau airport
Cayenne, French Guiana
Client: Cayenne Chamber of Commerce and Industry
Architects: Architecture Studio (M. Robain, R. Tisnado, J.-F. Bonne,
J.-F. Galmiche, A. Bretagnolle, R.-H. Arnaud)
Assistants: B. Mary, C. Gautié, F. Thiébault
Engineers: Séchaud & Bossuyt
Contractor: Baudin Chateauneuf
Consultants: B.-H. Vayssière (town planning), M. Sardou (aerodynamics),
D. Lucigny (economy)
Surface: 8,600 square metres
Competition, award-winning project
Delivery scheduled for 1996

26

Rehabilitation of an apartment building [27]
31, rue Boissy d'Anglas—75008 Paris
Client: J.-M. Levet
Architects: Architecture Studio (M. Robain, R. Tisnado, J.-F. Bonne,
J.-F. Galmiche, A. Bretagnolle, R.-H. Arnaud) D. Studio (S. Petit)
Assistant: G. Sanchez
Delivery: 1991

27

International conference centre
  Paris
  Client: Ministry of External Relations
  Architects: Architecture Studio (M. Robain, R. Tisnado, J.-F. Bonne,
  J.-F. Galmiche, A. Bretagnolle, R.-H. Arnaud)
  Assistants: D. Lesbegueris, S. Planchez, F. Rabiet
  Consultant: F. Seigneur
  Competition

*Arènes High School
  Toulouse
  Client: Midi-Pyrénées Region
  Architects: Architecture Studio (M. Robain, R. Tisnado, J.-F. Bonne,
  J.-F. Galmiche, A. Bretagnolle, R.-H. Arnaud)
  Assistants: R. Ayache, J. Davis, S. Planchez, P. Dutertre, C. Poulissen
  Engineers: O.T.H. Sud Ouest
  Contractor: Bisseuil
  Consultant: E. Vivié (acoustics)
  Surface: 15,000 square metres
  Competition by invitation, award-winning project
  Delivery: 1991

French pavilion for the World Fair [28]
  Seville, Spain
  Client: French company for the world fair in Seville
  Architects: Architecture Studio (M. Robain, R. Tisnado, J.-F. Bonne,
  J.-F. Galmiche, A. Bretagnolle, R.-H. Arnaud)
  Assistants: R. Ayache, L. Johnsson, M. Gautrand
  Surface: 10,000 square metres
  Competition

28

***Scenography for the
"Paris and the daguerreotype" exhibition**
  Carnavalet Museum, Paris
  Client: City of Paris Directorate of Cultural Affairs
  Architects: Architecture Studio (M. Robain, R. Tisnado, J.-F. Bonne,
  J.-F. Galmiche, A. Bretagnolle, R.-H. Arnaud), D. Studio (S. Petit)
  Consultants: F. Reynaud, J. Schwartz, C. Tambrun
  Delivery: 1989

Edouard Vaillant Vocational High School [29]
  Boulogne-Billancourt
  Client: Île-de-France Regional Council
  Architects: Architecture Studio (M. Robain, R. Tisnado, J.-F. Bonne,
  J.-F. Galmiche, A. Bretagnolle, R.-H. Arnaud)
  Assistant: P. Comes
  Engineers: B.E.F.S.-T.E.C. Ingénierie
  Contractor: S.A.E.P.
  Surface: 9,000 square metres
  Design–building competition

International student village
  Lyons
  Client: Rhône-Alpes Region
  Architects: Architecture Studio (M. Robain, R. Tisnado, J.-F. Bonne,
  J.-F. Galmiche, A. Bretagnolle, R.-H. Arnaud)
  Assistants: D. Lesbegueris, M.-H. Maurette, D. Lapernon, J.-L. Frenoy
  Associated architects: Curtelin-Ricard & associates
  Engineers: Serete
  Consultant: E. Vivié (acoustics), J.-P. Chevalard (economy)
  Surface: 28,500 square metres
  Competition

29

Development of future district [30]
  Cergy-le-Haut
  Client: Public Development Corporation
  of the new town of Cergy-Pontoise
  Architects: Architecture Studio (M. Robain, R. Tisnado, J.-F. Bonne,
  J.-F. Galmiche, A. Bretagnolle, R.-H. Arnaud)
  Assistants: J.-C. Vilain, F. Rabiet
  Surface to be developed: 60 hectares

*European Patents Office
  The Hague, Netherlands
  Architects: Architecture Studio (M. Robain, R. Tisnado, J.-F. Bonne,
  J.-F. Galmiche, A. Bretagnolle, R.-H. Arnaud)
  Associated architect: Boyeroche
  Surface: 200,000 square metres
  International competition

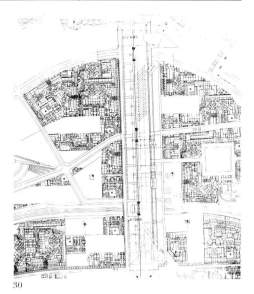
30

Congress centre [31]
  Tours
  Client: City of Tours
  Architects: Architecture Studio (M. Robain, R. Tisnado, J.-F. Bonne,
  J.-F. Galmiche, A. Bretagnolle, R.-H. Arnaud)
  Assistants: M. Gautrand, I. Hérault
  Consultants: M. Mimram (structure), Acora (scenography), E. Vivié (acoustics),
  Noble ingénierie (fluids), D. Lucigny (economy), M. Desvignes (landscape)
  Surface: 23,000 square metres
  Competition

31

Restructuring of the La Défense district [32]
  Paris-La-Défense
  Client: Secretariat of State for Major Works
  Architects: Architecture Studio (M. Robain, R. Tisnado, J.-F. Bonne,
  J.-F. Galmiche, A. Bretagnolle, R.-H. Arnaud)
  Assistants: J.-C. Vilain, P. Bona
  Consultant: B.-H. Vayssière (town planning)

*University residence
  4/6/8, rue Francis de Croisset—75018 Paris
  Client: S.A.G.I.
  Architects: Architecture Studio (M. Robain, R. Tisnado, J.-F. Bonne,
  J.-F. Galmiche, A. Bretagnolle, R.-H. Arnaud)
  Assistants: G. Gomez de Souza, J. Ledu, F. Magendie, F. Messier, B. Beissel von Gymnich,
  Engineers: Noble ingénierie
  Contractor: S.I.C.R.A.
  Consultants: D. Lucigny (economy), E. Vivié (acoustics)
  Surface: 11,000 square metres
  Competition, award-winning project
  Delivery scheduled for 1996

32

**Second project for the commemoration
of the Bicentenary of the Revolution** [33]
  Passerelle de Solférino, Paris
  Client: Lazzio Region, Rome
  Architects: Architecture Studio (M. Robain, R. Tisnado, J.-F. Bonne,
  J.-F. Galmiche, A. Bretagnolle, R.-H. Arnaud)
  Assistant: J.-C. Vilain
  Associate: U. Attardi (sculpture)

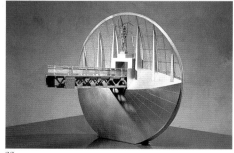
33

St George Seminary Church
  Francfurt-am-Main, Germany
  Client: St George Philosophical and Theological College
  Architects: Architecture Studio (M. Robain, R. Tisnado, J.-F. Bonne,
  J.-F. Galmiche, A. Bretagnolle, R.-H. Arnaud)
  Associated architect: C. Conrad
  Consultant: Father Labarrière
  Surface: 1,700 square metres
  International competition

1988

* "La City" business centre
    ZAC Louise Michel—25000 Besancon
    Client: Doubs Department Road and Building Infrastructure Corporation
    Architects: Architecture Studio (M. Robain, R. Tisnado, J.-F. Bonne,
    J.-F. Galmiche, A. Bretagnolle, R.-H. Arnaud)
    Assistants: P. Reibel, A. Bon
    Associated architect: P. Lamboley
    Engineers: O.T.E. Ingénierie
    Contractor: G.T.F.C.
    Consultant: D. Lucigny (economy)
    Surface: 35,000 square metres
    Competition, award-winning project
    Delivery scheduled for 2000

"Head" building of the
Pitié-Salpêtrière hospital complex [34]

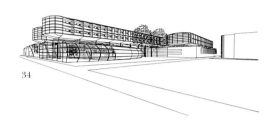

34

    Paris
    Client: Paris Health and Welfare Services
    Architects: Architecture Studio (M. Robain, R. Tisnado, J.-F. Bonne, J.-F. Galmiche)
    Assistants: A. Bretagnolle, R.-H. Arnaud, M. Cochet, D. Lapernon
    Engineers: Sogelerg
    Surface: 20,000 square metres
    Competition

*Student living centre
    Parc du Futuroscope 86000 Jaunay-Clan
    Client: O.P.D.H.L.M., Vienne Department
    Architects: Architecture Studio (M. Robain, R. Tisnado, J.-F. Bonne,
    J.-F. Galmiche, A. Bretagnolle, R.-H. Arnaud)
    Assistants: L. Pillaud, S. Petit
    Associated architect: F.-X. Désert
    Engineers: Bétom, Catalyse (home automation)
    Contractor: Bouyet
    Surface: 4,500 square metres
    Competition by invitation, award-winning project
    Delivery: 1989

*Canal+ headquarters
    Paris
    Client: Canal+
    Client nominee: Cogedim
    Architects: Architecture Studio (M. Robain, R. Tisnado, J.-F. Bonne, J.-F. Galmiche)
    Assistant: J.-C. Vilain
    Surface: 35,000 square metres
    International competition by invitation

*National Judo Institute
    Porte de Chatillon—75014 Paris
    Client: French Judo Federation
    Architects: Architecture Studio (M. Robain, R. Tisnado, J.-F. Bonne,
    J.-F. Galmiche, A. Bretagnolle, R.-H. Arnaud)
    Assistants: M. Gautrand, P. Bona, R. Djian, H. Wollensak, A. Bon
    Surface: 34,000 square metres
    Competition by invitation, award-winning project
    Delivery scheduled for 1996

Roubaix Euroteleport [35]
    Roubaix
    Client: S.E.M. of the north-eastern side of the Nord metropolis
    Architects: Architecture Studio (M. Robain, R. Tisnado, J.-F. Bonne,
    J.-F. Galmiche, A. Bretagnolle, R.-H. Arnaud)
    Assistants: I. Hérault, P. Robaglia, D. Lesbegueris
    Engineers: S.O.D.E.G.
    Consultant: S.C.E.T. Nord Pas-de-Calais
    Surface to be developed: 4 hectares
    Surface: 90,000 square metres in the long term

35

"Futura" business centre [(36)]
    Béthune
    Client: S.A.R.I.-S.E.E.R.I.
    Architects: Architecture Studio (M. Robain, R. Tisnado, J.-F. Bonne, J.-F. Galmiche)
    Assistants: M. Gautrand, I. Hérault, B. Vivien
    Engineers: Cotrasec
    Surface: 20,000 square metres

High school [(37)]
    Avignon
    Client: Provence-Côte d'Azur Region
    Architects: Architecture Studio (M. Robain, R. Tisnado, J.-F. Bonne, J.-F. Galmiche)
    Associated architect: M. Bernard
    Engineers: Beterem
    Contractor: René Jean & Anicet Martin
    Consultants: M. Sardou (aerodynamics), M. Rouch
    Surface: 12,000 square metres
    Design–building competition

Rehabilitation of the St Victor Hospital
    Amiens
    Client: Amiens General Hospital
    Architects: Architecture Studio (M. Robain, R. Tisnado, J.-F. Bonne, J.-F. Galmiche)
    Assistants: R.-H. Arnaud, L.-M. Fischer
    Engineers: Sodeteg Ingénierie
    Surface: 14,500 square metres
    Competition

Office building [(38)]
    Boulevard Masséna, Paris
    Client: S.E.M.A.P.A.
    Architects: Architecture Studio (M. Robain, R. Tisnado, J.-F. Bonne, J.-F. Galmiche)
    Surface: 3,500 square metres
    Competition

Berlin-Denkmal Oder
Denkmodel Project [(39)]
    Berlin
    Client: Berlin Senate, Aedes (Kristin Feireiss Galerie für Architektur)
    Architects: Architecture Studio (M. Robain, R. Tisnado, J.-F. Bonne, J.-F. Galmiche)
    Assistants: A. Bretagnolle, F. Roche
    Project exhibited in Berlin in 1988 and at the Arsenal Pavilion in 1989

First project for the commemoration
of the Bicentenary of the Revolution
    Pont des Arts, Paris
    Client: Lazzio Region, Rome
    Architects: Architecture Studio (M. Robain, R. Tisnado, J.-F. Bonne, J.-F. Galmiche)
    Assistant: O. Tossan
    Associate: U. Attardi (sculpture)

*Post office and mail sorting centre
    18/20, boulevard de la Chapelle—75018 Paris
    Client: Paris-Nord Post Office Directorate
    Architects: Architecture Studio (M. Robain, R. Tisnado, J.-F. Bonne,
    J.-F. Galmiche, A. Bretagnolle, R.-H. Arnaud)
    Assistant: N. Girard
    Engineers: O.T.H. Bâtiment
    Contractor: Hervé
    Surface: 11,000 square metres
    Competition, award-winning project
    Delivery: 1993

36

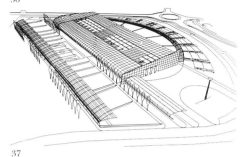

37

38

39

Chronological List of Buildings and Projects

*Fire station
136/140, rue Henri Barbusse—92230 Gennevilliers
Client: City of Paris, Police Headquarters
Architects: Architecture Studio (M. Robain, R. Tisnado, J.-F. Bonne,
J.-F. Galmiche, A. Bretagnolle, R.-H. Arnaud)
Assistants: R. Ayache, D. Stanley, J. Davis, M. Gautrand
Engineers: Technip Seri Construction
Contractor: Pizzarotti
Surface: 12,000 square metres
Competition, award-winning project
Delivery scheduled for 1995

High school [40]
La Roche-sur-Yon
Client: Pays-de-Loire Region
Architects: Architecture Studio (M. Robain, R. Tisnado, J.-F. Bonne, J.-F. Galmiche)
Assistants: A. Bretagnolle, R.-H. Arnaud, L. Jouben
Surface: 11,000 square metres
Competition

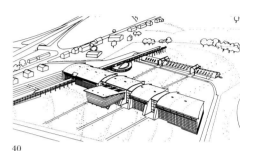

40

Parc de Passy Development [41]
Paris
Client: Ministry of Road and Building Infrastructure, Housing, Town Planning and
Transport, Directorate of Architecture and Town Planning
Client associate: S.E.R.E.S.
Architects: Architecture Studio (M. Robain, R. Tisnado, J.-F. Bonne, J.-F. Galmiche)
Assistant: F. Roche
Consultant: A. Richert (landscape)
Surface: 49,000 square metres
Promotion competition

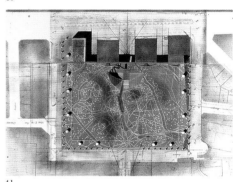

41

Old people's apartments and home [42]
Rue Furtado-Heine, Paris
Client: City of Paris, R.I.V.P.
Architects: Architecture Studio (M. Robain, R. Tisnado, J.-F. Bonne, J.-F. Galmiche)
Assistants: A. Bretagnolle, J.-C. Vilain
Surface: 18,000 square metres
Competition

Vocational high school
Cran-Gevrier
Client: Rhône-Alpes Region
Architects: Architecture Studio (M. Robain, R. Tisnado, J.-F. Bonne, J.-F. Galmiche)
Assistants: F. Gruson, L. Joubert
Associated architects: Bellon, Paczowski, Sobotta
Engineering: Technip
Surface: 19,000 square metres
Competition

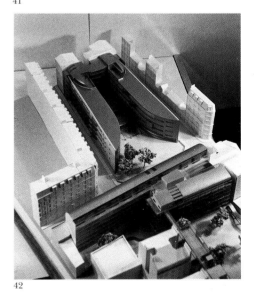

42

Hotelier high school [43]
Villers-les-Nancy
Client: Nancy Urban District
Architects: Architecture Studio (M. Robain, R. Tisnado, J.-F. Bonne, J.-F. Galmiche)
Assistants: F. Roche, L. Joubert, D. Lesbegueris, A. Moatti, F. Neubauer, J.-C. Vilain
Associated architects: J. Sebillote, J.-F. Badoc
Engineering: O.T.H. Est
Consultant: J.-P. Gauthier
Surface: 20,000 square metres
Competition

43

**Rue de Belleville
apartment building** [44]
> Paris
> Client: R.I.V.P.
> Architects: Architecture Studio (M. Robain, R. Tisnado, J.-F. Bonne,
> J.-F. Galmiche, A. Bretagnolle, R.-H. Arnaud)
> Assistants: S. Petit, M.-D. Danel
> Surface: 3,000 square metres

Law Courts
> Bordeaux
> Client: Ministry of Justice
> Architects: Architecture Studio (M. Robain, R. Tisnado, J.-F. Bonne, J.-F. Galmiche)
> Assistants: J.-C. Vilain, L. Joubert
> Surface: 15,000 square metres
> Competition

High school
> Jouée-les-Tours
> Client: Centre Region
> Architects: Architecture Studio (M. Robain, R. Tisnado, J.-F. Bonne, J.-F. Galmiche)
> Assistants: R.-H. Arnaud, L. Joubert
> Engineering: S.E.T.I.E.M., M. Robustelli
> Consultant: E. Vivié (acoustics)
> Surface: 10,000 square metres
> Competition

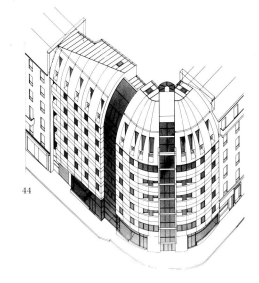
44

1987

Biotechnology Research Centre
> Sofia, Bulgaria
> Architects: Architecture Studio (M. Robain, R. Tisnado, J.-F. Bonne, J.-F. Galmiche)
> Assistant: F. Gruson
> Engineering: Technip
> Surface: 40,000 square metres
> Consultancy

Rebuilding of the Hôtel-Dieu [45]
> Castres
> Client: Hôtel-Dieu de Castres
> Architects: Architecture Studio (M. Robain, R. Tisnado, J.-F. Bonne, J.-F. Galmiche)
> Assistants: A. Bretagnolle, L. Joubed, M.-D. Danel
> Associated architects: R. Sagnes, J.-M. Pettes
> Engineering: O.T.C.E.
> Surface: 12,000 square metres
> Competition, award-winning project

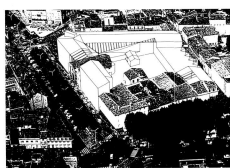
45

Rebuilding of vocational high school [46]
> Vaux-le-Pénil
> Client: Île-de-France Region
> Architects: Architecture Studio (M. Robain, R. Tisnado, J.-F. Bonne, J.-F. Galmiche)
> Assistants: D. Lesbegueris, L. Joubert
> Surface: 12,000 square metres
> Competition

**Rodin Museum extension
and redevelopment** [47]
> Paris
> Architects: Architecture Studio (M. Robain, R. Tisnado, J.-F. Bonne, J.-F. Galmiche)
> Assistants: A. Bretagnolle, R. Fourrier
> Surface: 4,500 square metres
> Competition

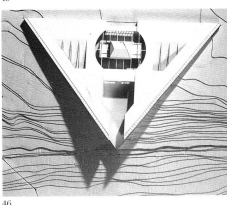
46

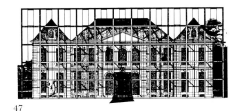
47

Chronological List of Buildings and Projects

Rebuilding of vocational high school [48]
Juvisy
Client: Île-de-France Regional Council
Architects: Architecture Studio (M. Robain, R. Tisnado, J.-F. Bonne, J.-F. Galmiche)
Assistants: F. Gruson, A. Jahan, L. Joubert
Surface: 11,000 square metres
Competition

Children's outdoor activity centre
Mandres-Les-Roses
Client: Deposit and Consignment Office
Architects: Architecture Studio (M. Robain, R. Tisnado, J.-F. Bonne, J.-F. Galmiche)
Assistant: A. Bretagnolle

Îlot Saint-Ange Development
Paris
Client: S.C.I.C.A.M.O.
Architects: Architecture Studio (M. Robain, R. Tisnado, J.-F. Bonne, J.-F. Galmiche)
Assistants: A. Bretagnolle, S. de Bokay, A. Moatti
Surface: 13,500 square metres
Competition

Rue Lesage apartment building
Paris
Client: R.I.V.P.
Architects: Architecture Studio (M. Robain, R. Tisnado, J.-F. Bonne, J.-F. Galmiche)
Assistant: A. Bretagnolle
Surface: 2,200 square metres

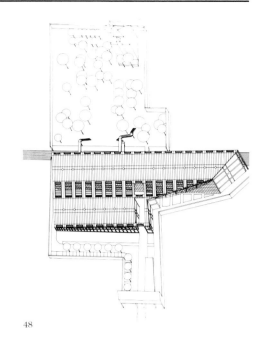

48

**Offices for the Communications Branch
of the Société Générale**
Boulevard des Capucines, Paris
Client: Société Générale
Architects: Architecture Studio (M. Robain, R. Tisnado, J.-F. Bonne,
J.-F. Galmiche), D. Studio (S. Petit)
Surface: 1,500 square metres
Delivery: 1988

Elderly persons' residence [49]
Meudon
Client: A.P.R.I.S.A.
Architects: Architecture Studio (M. Robain, R. Tisnado, J.-F. Bonne, J.-F. Galmiche)
Assistant: F. Gruson
Consultant: G. Piolle
Surface: 3,600 square metres
Competition

Second Daumesnil viaduct development project
Paris
Client: City of Paris, S.E.M.E.A.E.S.T.
Architects: Architecture Studio (M. Robain, R. Tisnado, J.-F. Bonne, J.-F. Galmiche)
Assistant: R. Fourrier
Surface: 11,500 square metres
Competition

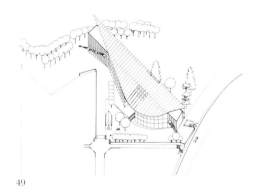

49

*Citadel University
Quai Freycinet—59140 Dunkirk
Client: Dunkirk Urban Community
Architects: Architects: Architecture Studio (M. Robain, R. Tisnado, J.-F. Bonne,
J.-F. Galmiche, A. Bretagnolle, R.-H. Arnaud)
Assistants: M. Gautrand, L. Joubert
Engineering: Serete, O.T.H. Nord
Contractor: Norpac, S.T.T. Dumez
Surface: 15,000 square metres
Competition, award-winning project
Delivery: 1990

1986

*French Embassy
Al Khuwair quarter, Muscat, Sultanate of Oman
Client: Ministry of Foreign Affairs
Architects: Architecture Studio (M. Robain, R. Tisnado, J.-F. Bonne, J.-F. Galmiche)
Assistants: D. Lesbegueris, A. Moati, S. Petit
Engineering: Technip
Contractor: Glauser International
Surface: 4,600 square metres
Delivery: 1989

Bastide district development (50)
Bordeaux
Client: City of Bordeaux
Architects: Architecture Studio (M. Robain, R. Tisnado, J.-F. Bonne, J.-F. Galmiche)
Assistant: C. Pueyo
Consultant: Arc en Rêve
Proposal for the City of Bordeaux

50

Extended care centre
Hospital, Kremlin-Bicêtre
Client: Health and Welfare Services
Architects: Architecture Studio (M. Robain, R. Tisnado, J.-F. Bonne, J.-F. Galmiche)
Assistant: F. Gruson
Engineering: O.T.H.
Surface: 11,000 square metres
Competition

State Security Police
(C.R.S.) barracks (51)
Darnétal
Client: Ministry of the Interior, S.G.A.P. of Lille
Architects: Architecture Studio (M. Robain, R. Tisnado, J.-F. Bonne, J.-F. Galmiche)
Assistant: J. Jacquiod
Engineering: O.T.H. Bâtiment
Surface: 7,000 square metres
Competition

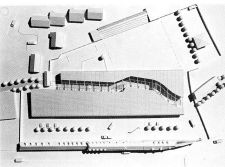

51

Development of central business district (52)
Arcachon
Client: City of Arcachon
Architects: Architecture Studio (M. Robain, R. Tisnado, J.-F. Bonne, J.-F. Galmiche)
Assistants: R.-H. Arnaud, D. Harding
Consultancy

Facade for a hotel
Rue Trousseau, Paris
Client: Groupe Maison Familiale
Architects: Architecture Studio (M. Robain, R. Tisnado, J.-F. Bonne, J.-F. Galmiche)
Assistant: M. Gautrand
Delivery: 1988

Boulevard Faidherbe apartments
and activities
Amiens
Client: O.P.A.C., Amiens
Architects: Architecture Studio (M. Robain, R. Tisnado, J.-F. Bonne, J.-F. Galmiche)
Associated architect: C. Conrad
Surface: 12,000 square metres
Competition, award-winning project

52

Rebuilding of retirement home [53]
  Donzy
  Client: Donzy Retirement Home
  Architects: Architecture Studio (M. Robain, R. Tisnado, J.-F. Bonne,
  J.-F. Galmiche, A. Bretagnolle, R.-H. Arnaud)
  Assistants: M.-D. Danel, F. Gruson, S. Burger
  Engineering: Igou Structure, Noble ingénierie
  Surface: 5,000 square metres
  Competition, award-winning project
  Delivery: 1991

*Our Lady of the Ark of the Covenant Church
  Rue de la Procession—75015 Paris
  Client: Diocesan Association of Paris, Archbishopric of Paris
  Architects: Architecture Studio (M. Robain, R. Tisnado, J.-F. Bonne,
  J.-F. Galmiche, A. Bretagnolle, R.-H. Arnaud, L.-M. Fischer)
  Assistants: P. Sardin, R. Fourrier, F. Gruson
  Engineering: Noble ingénierie
  Consultants: A.T.E.C. (economy), G. Berne (lighting), Casso & Cie (safety),
  E. Vivié (acoustics)
  Surface: 1,400 square metres
  Delivery scheduled for 1996

*High School of the Future
  Parc du Futuroscope—86000 Jaunay-Clan
  Client: Poitou-Charentes Region
  Architects: Architecture Studio (M. Robain, R. Tisnado, J.-F. Bonne, J.-F. Galmiche)
  Assistants: R.-H. Arnaud, P. Balch
  Associated architect: F.-X. Désert
  Engineering: Technip Seri Construction
  Contractor: S.A.E.
  Surface: 19,000 square metres
  Competition, award-winning project
  Delivery: 1987

School complex
  Montigny-le-Bretonneux
  Client: Public Development Corporation of the new town
  of St-Quentin-en-Yvelines
  Architects: Architecture Studio (M. Robain, R. Tisnado, J.-F. Bonne, J.-F. Galmiche)
  Assistant: F. Gruson
  Engineering: Arcoba
  Surface: 3,500 square metres
  Competition

E.l.f. automated storage building [54]
  Rouen
  Client: E.l.f.-Aquitaine Company
  Architects: Architecture Studio (M. Robain, R. Tisnado, J.-F. Bonne,
  J.-F. Galmiche, F.-X. Désert)
  Assistant: R.-H. Arnaud
  Engineering: Technip Seri Construction
  Surface: 16,000 square metres
  Consultancy

1985

National School of Ballet [55]
  Marseille
  Client: City of Marseille, Ballet National de Marseille, Roland Petit
  Architects: Architecture Studio (M. Robain, R. Tisnado, J.-F. Bonne,
  J.-F. Galmiche, F.-X. Désert)
  Assistant: F. Gruson
  Surface: 5,700 square metres
  Competition

53

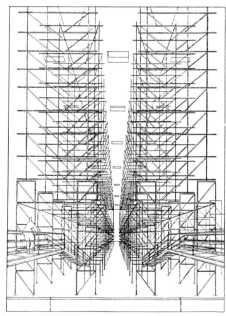

54

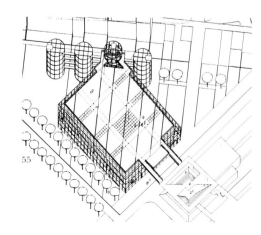

55

Development of the Saint-Martin-de-Porrès Chapel

37, rue Jacques Ibert—75017 Paris
Client: Les chantiers du Cardinal, Archbishopric of Paris
Architects: Architecture Studio (M. Robain, R. Tisnado, J.-F. Bonne, J.-F. Galmiche, F.-X. Désert)
Assistants: O. Boiron, S. de Bokay
Surface: 70 square metres
Delivery: 1985

Psychiatric centre

Calais
Client: Calais Departmental Directorate of Road and Building Infrastructure, Calais General Hospital
Architects: Architecture Studio (M. Robain, R. Tisnado, J.-F. Bonne, J.-F. Galmiche, F.-X. Désert)
Assistant: O. Boiron
Surface: 3,700 square metres
Competition

Development of children's workshop [56]

Georges Pompidou Centre—75004 Paris
Client: Georges Pompidou Centre
Architects: Architecture Studio (M. Robain, R. Tisnado, J.-F. Bonne, J.-F. Galmiche, F.X. Désert)
Assistant: S. de Bokay
Surface: 250 square metres
Delivery: 1986

56

Courvoisier automated storage building [57]

Foussignac
Client: Courvoisier
Architects: Architecture Studio (M. Robain, R. Tisnado, J.-F. Bonne, J.-F. Galmiche, F.-X. Désert)
Assistant: R.-H. Arnaud
Engineering: Serete
Surface: 9,000 square metres
Competition by invitation, award-winning project

57

Museum of science and technology

Poitiers
Client: City of Poitiers
Architects: Architecture Studio (M. Robain, R. Tisnado, J.-F. Bonne, J.-F. Galmiche, F.-X. Désert)
Assistants: R. Fourrier, C. Pueyo
Engineering: Sodeteg
Surface: 1,600 square metres
Competition by invitation

Law Courts (Cité Judiciaire)

Clermont-Ferrand
Client: Ministry of Justice
Architects: Architecture Studio (M. Robain, R. Tisnado, J.-F. Bonne, J.-F. Galmiche, F.-X. Désert)
Assistant: A. Bretagnolle
Consultant: T. Grumbach
Surface: 20,000 square metres
Competition by invitation

World of Work record office [58]

Roubaix
Client: Ministry of Culture, City of Roubaix
Architects: Architecture Studio (M. Robain, R. Tisnado, J.-F. Bonne, J.-F. Galmiche, F.-X. Désert)
Assistants: C. Pueyo, F. Magendie
Engineering: Technip Seri Construction
Consultant: M. Hamont
Surface: 24,000 square metres
Competition

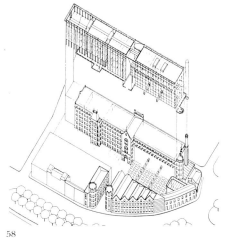

58

Chronological List of Buildings and Projects

19th arrondissement municipal school of music [59]
Paris
Client: City of Paris
Architects: Architecture Studio (M. Robain, R. Tisnado, J.-F. Bonne, J.-F. Galmiche, F.-X. Désert)
Engineering: B.E.T.F.
Consultants: E. Vivie, M. Castellengo, Simsen (acoustics)
Surface: 1,800 square metres
Competition by invitation

59

Vocational high school
Ribecourt-Dreslincourt
Client: Ministry of National Education
Architects: Architecture Studio (M. Robain, R. Tisnado, J.-F. Bonne, J.-F. Galmiche, F.-X. Désert)
Assistants: R. Koltirine, I. Richard
Engineering: B.E.T.F.
Consultants: Casso-Gaudin (safety), M. Castellengo (acoustics)
Surface: 7,000 square metres
Competition by invitation

Cordon-Jaurès apartment building
Saint-Ouen
Client: S.E.M.I.S.O.
Architects: Architecture Studio (M. Robain, R. Tisnado, J.-F. Bonne, J.-F. Galmiche, A. Bretagnolle, R.-H. Arnaud)
Assistants: N. Mecattaf, F. Janneau, F. Magendie
Associated architect: P. Soria
Engineering: B.E.R.I.M.
Delivery: 1992

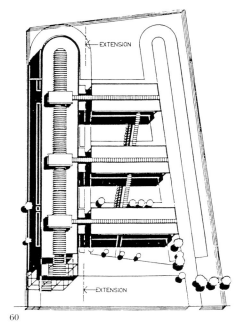
60

Megat [60]
Cesson-Sévigné
Client: Telecommunications Directorate
Architects: Architecture Studio (M. Robain, R. Tisnado, J.-F. Bonne, J.-F. Galmiche, F.-X. Désert)
Assistant: F. Gruson
Engineering: O.T.H.
Surface: 3,000 square metres
Competition by invitation

Sainte-Croix quarter redevelopment [61]
Buxerolles
Client: Commune of Buxerolles
Architects: Architecture Studio (M. Robain, R. Tisnado, J.-F. Bonne, J.-F. Galmiche, F.-X. Désert)
Engineering: Sodeteg
Consultant: A. Chemetoff
Surface to be developed: 20 hectares
Competition

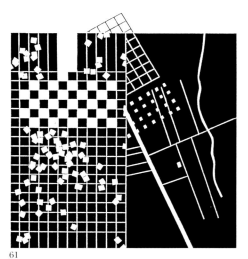
61

Rehabilitation of apartments [62]
Belfort
Client: O.P.D.H.L.M., Belfort
Architects: Architecture Studio (M. Robain, R. Tisnado, J.-F. Bonne, J.-F. Galmiche, F.-X. Désert)
Engineering: Santini & Bechler
Surface: 480 square metres
Delivery: 1985

62

U.T.A. Head office [63]
   Le Bourget
   Client: U.T.A.
   Architects: Architecture Studio (M. Robain, R. Tisnado, J.-F. Bonne,
   J.-F. Galmiche, F.-X. Désert)
   Assistants: A. Bretagnolle, R. Fourrier
   Surface: 20,000 square metres
   Competition by invitation

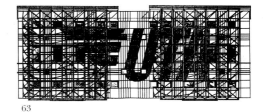

63

1984

*Apartment building
   106, rue du Château des Rentiers—75013 Paris
   Client: Habitat Social Francais
   Architects: Architecture Studio (M. Robain, R. Tisnado, J.-F. Bonne, J.-F. Galmiche)
   Assistants: R. Fourrier, F. Magendie
   Contractor: Boschetti-Wilhem
   Surface: 1,300 square metres
   Delivery: 1986

"Suburbs 89" [64]
   Belfort
   Client: City of Belfort
   Architects: Architecture Studio (M. Robain, R. Tisnado, J.-F. Bonne,
   J.-F. Galmiche, F.-X. Désert)
   Assistant: D. Harding

64

"Suburbs 89" [65]
   Grand-Charmond
   Client: City of Grand-Charmond
   Architects: Architecture Studio (M. Robain, R. Tisnado, J.-F. Bonne,
   J.-F. Galmiche, F.-X. Désert)
   Assistant: D. Harding

65

"Suburbs 89"
   Vesoul
   Client: City of Vesoul
   Architects: Architecture Studio (M. Robain, R. Tisnado, J.-F. Bonne,
   J.-F. Galmiche, F.-X. Désert)
   Assistant: D. Harding

Stimuli: A study on Paris [66]
   Architects: Architecture Studio (M. Robain, R. Tisnado, J.-F. Bonne,
   J.-F. Galmiche, F.-X. Désert)
   Assistants: J.-C. Vilain, R.-H. Arnaud, R. Fourrier, C. Pueyo
   Consultant: Avenir Publicité
   Proposal published by Editions Champs Vallon, 1987

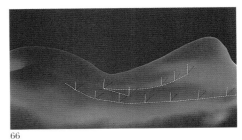

66

Lorraine Regional Audit Office
   Épinal
   Client: Ministry of the Economy and Finance
   Architects: Architecture Studio (M. Robain, R. Tisnado, J.-F. Bonne,
   J.-F. Galmiche, F.-X. Désert)
   Assistant: R. Fourrier
   Engineering: G.R.I.C.
   Surface: 3,000 square metres
   Competition by invitation

First project for the Daumesnil viaduct [67]
   Paris
   Architects: Architecture Studio (M. Robain, R. Tisnado, J.-F. Bonne,
   J.-F. Galmiche)
   Assistants: R.-H. Arnaud, R. Fourrier, C. Pueyo
   Proposal

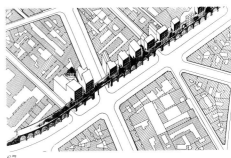

67

1983

French Embassy [68]
    Mexico City, Mexico
    Client: Ministry of External Relations
    Architects: Architecture Studio (M. Robain, R. Tisnado, J.-F. Bonne,
    J.-F. Galmiche, F.-X. Désert)
    Engineering: S.E.T.E.C. Bâtiment
    Competition

Bougenel district apartment building [69]
    Belfort
    Client: A.U.T.B.
    Architects: Architecture Studio (M. Robain, R. Tisnado, J.-F. Bonne,
    J.-F. Galmiche, F.-X. Désert)
    Assistants: P. Delage
    Engineering: Arcoba
    Surface: 9,000 square metres
    Competition by invitation

Psychiatric services,
Corentin Celton Hospital
    Issy-les-Moulineaux
    Client: Health and Welfare Services
    Architects: Architecture Studio (M. Robain, R. Tisnado, J.-F. Bonne,
    J.-F. Galmiche, F.-X. Désert)
    Engineering: S.E.T.E.C. Bâtiment
    Consultant: Dr Roubier
    Surface: 3,500 square metres
    Competition by invitation

Bastille Opera House [70]
    Paris
    Client: Ministry of Culture
    Architects: Architecture Studio (M. Robain, R. Tisnado, J.-F. Bonne,
    J.-F. Galmiche, F.-X. Désert)
    Consultant: J. le Marquet (scenography)
    International competition

* **"Tête de la Défense"**
    Paris
    Client: Public Development Corporation of the Défense Quarter
    Architects: Architecture Studio (M. Robain, R. Tisnado, J.-F. Bonne,
    J.-F. Galmiche, F.-X. Désert) and J. Nouvel, J.-M. Ibos, D. Laroque
    Engineering: S.E.G.I.C. Ingénierie
    Consultants: J. le Marquet (scenography), F. Seigneur
    Surface: 150,000 square metres
    International competition,
    project awarded second place

Renovation of the Espace Saint-Pierre
    Clermont-Ferrand
    Client: City Council of Clermont-Ferrand, Puy de Dôme Department Directorate of
    Road and Building Infrastructure
    Architects: Architecture Studio (M. Robain, R. Tisnado, J.-F. Bonne,
    J.-F. Galmiche, F.-X. Désert)
    Competition

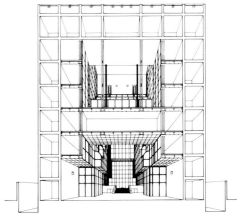

68

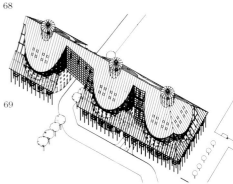

69

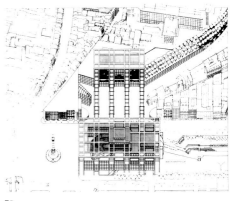

70

1982

Ministry of Finance [71]
  Paris
  Client: Ministry of Finance
  Architects: Architecture Studio (M. Robain, R. Tisnado, J.-F. Bonne,
  J.-F. Galmiche, F.-X. Désert)
  Associated architects: M. Gravayat, C. Hauvette
  Consultant: J. Séguéla
  Award-winning competition

**Completion of the Jussieu
university campus**
  Paris
  Client: S.C.A.R.I.F.
  Architects: Architecture Studio (M. Robain, R. Tisnado, J.-F. Bonne,
  J.-F. Galmiche, F.-X. Désert) and J. Nouvel, G. Lezenes, P. Soria

Palace for Prince Abdullah AI Faisal [72]
  Jeddah, Saudi Arabia
  Client: Prince Abdullah Al Faisal
  Architects: Architecture Studio (M. Robain, R. Tisnado, J.-F. Bonne,
  J.-F. Galmiche, F.-X. Désert)
  Consultant: Idea Center
  Surface: 1,600 square metres

Palace for Prince Naïf [73]
  Jeddah, Saudi Arabia
  Client: Prince Naïf Bin Abdulazziz
  Architects: Architecture Studio (M. Robain, R. Tisnado, J.-F. Bonne,
  J.-F. Galmiche, F.-X. Désert)
  Consultant: Idea Center
  Surface: 12,000 square metres

Live-in factory
  2ter, passage des Marais—75020 Paris
  Client: S.C.I. Passage des Marais
  Architects: Architecture Studio (M. Robain, R. Tisnado, J.-F. Bonne,
  J.-F. Galmiche, F.-X. Désert)
  Assistant: R. Fourrier
  Surface: 900 square metres
  Delivery: 1983

**Renovation of the Sainte-Anne
Hospital psychiatric services** [74]
  Paris
  Client: Sainte-Anne Hospital Complex
  Architects: Architecture Studio (M. Robain, R. Tisnado, J.-F. Bonne,
  J.-F. Galmiche, F.-X. Désert)
  Engineering: O.T.H. Bâtiment
  Surface: 6,000 square metres
  Competition by invitation, award-winning project

Humanisation of old people's home
  6, rue des Augustins—86500 Montmorillon
  Client: Montmorillon Hospital
  Architects: Architecture Studio (M. Robain, R. Tisnado, J.-F. Bonne,
  J.-F. Galmiche, F.-X. Désert)
  Surface: 1,200 square metres
  Delivery: 1984

*Kindergarten and primary school
  10, rue Mouraud—75020 Paris
  Client: City of Paris
  Architects: Architecture Studio (M. Robain, R. Tisnado, J.-F. Bonne,
  J.-F. Galmiche, F.-X. Désert)
  Engineering: S.E.T.E.C. Bâtiment
  Contractor: Nord France
  Surface: 5,800 square metres
  Competition by invitation, award-winning project
  Delivery: 1985

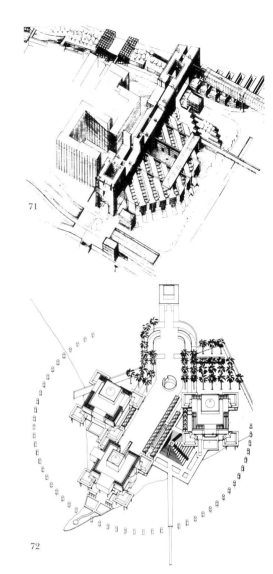

71

72

73

74

*Apartment building
>16, rue Domrémy—75013 Paris
>Client: Habitat Social Francais
>Architects: Architecture Studio (M. Robain, R. Tisnado, J.-F. Bonne,
>J.-F. Galmiche, F.-X. Désert)
>Assistant: R. Fourrier
>Surface: 1,700 square metres
>Delivery: 1984

S.f.e.n.a. Technical Research
Centre extension
>Chatellerault
>Client: S.f.e.n.a.
>Architects: Architecture Studio (M. Robain, R. Tisnado, J.-F. Bonne,
>J.-F. Galmiche, F.-X. Désert)
>Engineering: Serete
>Surface: 4,000 square metres
>Competition by invitation

1981

*Institute of the Arab World
>1, rue des Fossés Saint-Bernard—75005 Paris
>Client: Institute of the Arab World
>Architects: Architecture Studio (M. Robain, R. Tisnado, J.-F. Bonne,
>J.-F. Galmiche) and J. Nouvel, P. Soria, G. Lezenes
>Assistants: A. Robain, J.-J. Raynaud, P. Debard, A. Rispal, J.-L. Bernard
>Engineering: S.E.T.E.C. Bâtiment
>Consultants: Z. Zaïdan (consultant architect), G. Grandguillaume,
>J. Lemarquet, M. Seban (scenography), F. Seigneur (interior design),
>P.-M. Jacquot (plastic artist), L. Fruitet (consultant engineer),
>Light Design (museum lighting),A. Richert (landscape), Sery-Betrand (economy),
>Casso-Gaudin (safety)
>Surface: 27,000 square metres
>Competition by invitation, award-winning project
>Delivery: 1987
>Équerre d'Argent Award in 1988, Aga Khan Award in 1989

*Tihama cultural centre
>Jeddah, Saudi Arabia
>Client: Tihama
>Architects: Architecture Studio (M. Robain, R. Tisnado, J.-F. Bonne,
>J.-F. Galmiche, F.-X. Désert)
>Engineering: O.T.H. International
>Consultants: J. Lemarquet (scenography), Idea Center
>Surface: 30,000 square metres
>International competition by invitation

Town Hall [75]
>Savigny-le-Temple
>Client: Public Development Corporation
>of the new town of Melun Sénart
>Architects: Architecture Studio (M. Robain, R. Tisnado, J.-F. Bonne,
>J.-F. Galmiche, F.-X. Désert)
>Assistant: D. Harding
>Surface: 2,500 square metres
>Competition by invitation

75

*Renovation of facades
on the Boulevard de Courcelles
>9, boulevard de Courcelles—75008 Paris
>Client: Public company for the Rue de Monceau buildings
>Architects: Architecture Studio (M. Robain, R. Tisnado, J.-F. Bonne,
>J.-F. Galmiche, F.-X. Désert)
>Assistants: A. Robain, P. Debard
>Engineering: Ecotrab
>Delivery: 1984

*Héraud residence
Chasseneuil-du-Poitou
Client: Mr and Mrs Héraud
Architects: Architecture Studio (M. Robain, R. Tisnado, J.-F. Bonne,
J.-F. Galmiche, F.-X. Désert)
Surface: 210 square metres
Delivery: 1983

1980

Central business district development
Bavilliers
Client: S.O.D.E.B.-A.U.T.B.
Architects: Architecture Studio (M. Robain, R. Tisnado, J.-F. Bonne,
J.-F. Galmiche, F.-X. Désert)
Associated architect: D. Schlachter Cler
Engineering: G.R.I.C.
Competition by invitation

Baths residence
La Roche Posay
Client: C.O.R.E.V.A.
Architects: Architecture Studio (M. Robain, R. Tisnado, J.-F. Bonne,
J.-F. Galmiche, F.-X. Désert)
Surface: 9,300 square metres

Solar house
Client: Ministry of Roads and Building Infrastructure
Architects: Architecture Studio (M. Robain, R. Tisnado, J.-F. Bonne,
J.-F. Galmiche, F.-X. Désert)
Assistant: D. Harding
Engineering: Serete Entreprise Dumez
Contractor: Dumez
Consultant: ELF-Aquitaine
Surface: 90 to 130 square metres
"5,000 solar houses" competition, award-winning project

Holiday centre
Nouans-le-Fuzelier
Client: Commune of Nouans-le-Fuzelier, C.R.E.P.A.H.
Architects: Architecture Studio (M. Robain, R. Tisnado, J.-F. Bonne,
J.-F. Galmiche, F.-X. Désert)
Assistant: D. Harding
Engineering: O.T.H. Habitation
Surface: 1,200 square metres
Competition by invitation

**Science and technology museum
and Parc de la Villette development** [76]
Paris
Client: Parc de la Villette Corporation
Architects: Architecture Studio (M. Robain, R. Tisnado, J.-F. Bonne,
J.-F. Galmiche, F.-X. Désert)
Engineering: O.T.H. Bâtiment
Consultants: F. Barré, P. Colombot
Competition by invitation

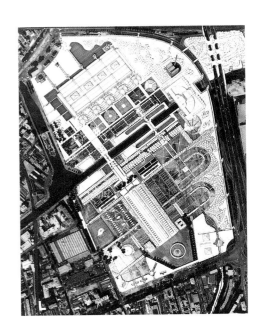

Saint-Nicolas primary school
Montmorillon
Client: Commune of Montmorillon
Architects: Architecture Studio (M. Robain, R. Tisnado, J.-F. Bonne,
J.-F. Galmiche, F.-X. Désert)
Engineering: C.E.T.E.B.
Surface: 450 square metres
Delivery: 1982

Conference hall
Ligugé
Client: Mutuelle de Poitiers
Architects: Architecture Studio (M. Robain, R. Tisnado, J.-F. Bonne,
J.-F. Galmiche, F.-X. Désert)
Assistant: L. Tournoux
Surface: 1,500 square metres

1979

Directorate of Departmental Infrastructure [77]
Poitiers
Client: Departmental Directorate of Road and Building Infrastructure, Poitiers
Architects: Architecture Studio (M. Robain, R. Tisnado, J.-F. Galmiche,
F.-X. Désert) and J. Nouvel, G. Lezenes
Assistants: J.-F. Bonne, M. Vitart
Engineering: O.T.H. Habitation
Consultant: F. Seigneur
Surface: 11,000 square metres
Competition by invitation

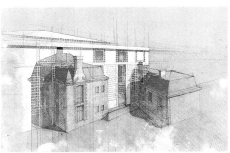

77

Apartments
Rue de l'As de Trèfle, Belfort
Client: O.P.D.H.L.M. de Belfort
Architects: Architecture Studio (M. Robain, R. Tisnado, J.-F. Galmiche)
Engineering: G.R.I.C.
Surface: 1,400 square metres
Competition by invitation, award-winning project
Delivery: 1983

Gasnier-Guy College
Chelles
Client: A.P.E.G. Association
Architects: Architecture Studio (M. Robain, R. Tisnado, J.-F. Galmiche, F.-X. Désert)
Engineering: Pingat
Consultant: M. Desthuilliers
Surface: 3,000 square metres
Competition by invitation, award-winning project
Delivery: 1980

*Architectural agency
10, rue Lacuée—75012 Paris
Client: Architecture Studio, J. Nouvel, P. Soria, G. Lezenes, Archigroup
Architects: Architecture Studio (M. Robain, R. Tisnado, J.-F. Galmiche)
Surface: 1,100 square metres
Delivery: 1980

78

1978

U.B.P. agency [78]
Rue de Fontenay—94300 Vincennes
Client: U.B.P.
Architects: Architecture Studio (M. Robain, R. Tisnado, J.-F. Galmiche, F.-X. Désert)
Engineering: Ecotrab
Delivery: 1979

Le Luzard Technical High School [79]
Val-Maubuée
Client: Public Development Corporation of the new town of
Marne-la-Vallée
Architects: Architecture Studio (M. Robain, R. Tisnado, J.-F. Galmiche, F.-X. Désert)
Engineering: Serete
Surface: 8,700 square metres
Competition by invitation

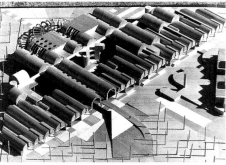

79

Hospital extension [80]
 2, rue Henri Dunan—86500 Montmorillon
 Client: Montmorillon Hospital
 Architects: Architecture Studio (M. Robain, R. Tisnado, J.-F. Galmiche, F.-X. Désert)
 Engineering: Pingat
 Surface: 1,300 square metres
 Delivery: 1981

Escolaco-Borda residence [81]
 Ascain
 Client: Mr and Mrs Magaz
 Architects: Architecture Studio (M. Robain, R. Tisnado, J.-F. Galmiche)
 Associated architect: A. Magaz
 Surface: 250 square metres
 Delivery: 1979

City buildings
 Cergy-Puiseux
 Client: Public Development Corporation
 of the new town of Cergy-Pontoise
 Architects: Architecture Studio (M. Robain, R. Tisnado, J.-F. Galmiche)
 Surface: 20,000 square metres
 Competition

80

81

1977

Opera House
 Abu Dhabi, Saudi Arabia
 Client: Emirate of Abu Dhabi, Ministry of Public Works
 Architects: Architecture Studio (M. Robain, R. Tisnado, J.-F. Galmiche)
 Engineering: O.T.H. International
 Consultant: E.P.T.A. International
 Surface: 65,000 square metres
 International competition by invitation

Antony town centre restructuring
 Antony
 Client: City of Antony, S.E.M.A.V.A.
 Architects: Architecture Studio (M. Robain, R. Tisnado, J.-F. Galmiche)
 Associated architects: V. de Baecque, Y.-J. Laval
 Engineering: O.T.H.
 Consultant: M. Goles
 Competition

82

1976

Decardes residence [82]
 Versailles
 Client: Mr and Mrs Decardes
 Architects: Architecture Studio (M. Robain, R. Tisnado, J.-F. Galmiche)
 Surface: 220 square metres
 Delivery: 1977

Chauvin residence [83]
 Ribellino, Corsica
 Client: Mr and Mrs Chauvin
 Architects: Architecture Studio (M. Robain, J.-F. Galmiche, Y.-J. Laval)
 Surface: 90 square metres
 Delivery: 1976

83

Bougenel quarter development
 Belfort
 Client: S.o.d.e.b.
 Architects: Architecture Studio (M. Robain, R. Tisnado, J.-F. Galmiche, Y.-J. Laval)
 Consultant: M. Goles
 Surface: 72,000 square metres
 Competition

1975

Apartments with
shared activity area
 Place de la Grande Goule—86000 Poitiers
 Client: O.p.d.h.l.m., Poitiers
 Architects: Architecture Studio (M. Robain, J.-F. Galmiche, Y.-J. Laval)
 Engineering: O.t.h. Habitation
 Consultant: P. Colombot (sociologist)
 Surface: 11,300 square metres
 Experimental construction competition
 Delivery: 1980

1974

Stud farm [84]
 Saint-Maclou
 Client: A. Clore
 Architects: Architecture Studio (M. Robain, J.-F. Galmiche)
 Delivery: 1974

84

1972

*Convalescent home
 Clamart
 Client: Our Lady of the Sacred Heart Hermitage
 Architect: Architecture Studio (M. Robain)
 Surface: 3,400 square metres
 Delivery: 1975
 First work

Awards, Exhibitions, Conferences and Teaching

Awards

Losange d'Argent
Île-de-France Regional Council
Rue Domrémy apartment building,
Paris 1985

Équerre d'Argent
Le Moniteur
Institute of the Arab World, Paris
1988

Aga Khan Award
The Aga Khan Award for Architecture
Institute of the Arab World, Paris
1989

Monographic Exhibitions

Architecture Studio Architecture
Architecture Gallery, Perpignan, France
1989

Town planning for all
Carcassonne 89 Association, Carcassonne,
France 1989

Architecture Studio
Instituto Nazionale di Architettura, Rome,
Italy 1988

Architecture Studio
Claude-Nicolas Ledoux Fondation, Arc
and Senans, France 1988

Architecture Studio
Attems Palace, Vienna, Austria 1987

Architecture Studio
Franco–Portuguese Institute, Lisbon,
Portugal 1987

Architecture Studio
Arc en Rêve, Bordeaux, France 1986
First monographic exhibition

Collective Exhibitions

Arquitectura francesa, 11 proyectos
Junta de Andalucia, Seville, Spain 1993

The design and the architect
Arsenal Pavilion, Paris, France 1992

**The city thresholds—Paris, from the
fortifications to the ring road**
Arsenal Pavilion, Paris, France 1992

Architettura e spazio sacro nella modernità
Venice Biennial Exhibition, Italy 1992

Ten years of architecture in Toulouse
Musée des Augustins, Toulouse,
France 1992

Arènes High School, Toulouse
Cogemip stand, International Architecture
Show, Paris, France
1990 (SIA Award for best stand)

Beaubourg 90—public orders
Georges Pompidou Centre, Paris,
France 1990

**An excellent generation of French
architects**
French Cultural Centre, Belgrade,
Yugoslavia 1990

French avant-garde architecture
The Art Institute, Chicago,
United States 1989

Paris–Berlin: architecture and utopia
Arsenal Pavilion, Paris, France 1989

**Sixtieth anniversary of the Technical
Office for the use of steel**
La Villette international conference
centre, Paris, France 1989

Paris: large projects, 1979/1989
US Custom House, New York,
United States 1988

Profiles in architecture & design
Royal Academy of Fine Arts, Stockholm,
Sweden 1988

Architectural Issues 88
French Institute of Architecture, Paris,
France 1988

Berlin-Denkmal oder Denkmodel
Aedes Gallery, Berlin, Germany 1988

French art-related architecture
French Cultural Centre, Helsinki,
Finland 1988

Vienne Department—public architectures
Departmental Directorate of the Vienne
Department Road and Building
Infrastructure, Poitiers, France 1988

**Franco–Scandinavian exhibition of
architecture and design**
Charlottenborg Museum, Copenhagen,
Denmark 1988

Art and arts, current issues and history
Venice Biennial Festival, Italy 1987

Institute of the Arab World
Micgoau, Athens, Greece 1986

Architecture and hospital design
French Institute of Architecture, Paris,
France 1985

New architectural pleasures
Georges Pompidou Centre, Paris,
France 1985

Institute of the Arab World
French Institute, Stockholm,
Sweden 1985

**Os grandes projectos arquitectonicos
en Paris**
Centre of Modern Art, Lisbon,
Portugal 1985

A tendency in French architecture
Academy of Fine Arts, Copenhagen,
Denmark 1984

3 large projects in Paris
French Institute of Architecture, Paris,
France 1983

A decade in architecture
Batimat, Paris, France 1983

**Extension of a medical clinic in
Montmorillon**
French Institute of Architecture, Paris,
France 1983

**Just for the heck of it, would you like to
take part in it?**
French Institute of Architecture, Paris,
France 1983

30 French architects exposition
2nd European assembly of architecture
students, Delft,
Netherlands 1982

Awards, Exhibitions, Conferences and Teaching

Institute of the Arab World
French Institute of Architecture, Paris, France 1981

First Paris Biennial Architecture Festival
Georges Pompidou Centre, Paris, France 1980

Building in old quarters
Grand Palais, Paris, France 1980

Conferences

Four measures: an European design forum
The Catholic University of America, Washington DC, United States 1994

Architecture Studio, projects and constructions
School of Architecture, Montreal, Canada 1993

Architecture Studio, projects and constructions
School of Architecture, Québec, 1993

Architecture Studio, projects and constructions
University of Houston, Texas, United States 1993

Architecture Studio, projects and constructions
French Cultural Centre, Hanoi, Vietnam 1993

Architecture Studio, projects and constructions
School of Architecture, Lyons, France 1993

Architecture Studio, city architecture detail
Università degli studi di Napoli, Naples, Italy 1992

Architecture Studio, projects and constructions
Fachschaft Architektur der TU-Wien, Vienna, Austria 1992

Architecture, city, culture and society
Facultad de Arquitectura y Urbanismo, Cordoba, Argentina 1992

Project manager/Client in European cities
Claude-Nicolas Ledoux Foundation, Arc and Senans, France 1992 Congress

Architecture and music
Pesmes, France
1992 Congress

Architecture Studio, projects and constructions
University of Wisconsin, United States 1990

Chicago versus Paris
Graham Foundation of Chicago, United States 1990 Congress

Architecture Studio, projects and constructions
Blacksburg School of Architecture, Virginia, United States 1989

Architecture Studio
Architecture gallery, Perpignan, France 1989

High technology in the service of architecture
Technological Institute of art, architecture and town planning, Tunis, Tunisia 1989

Architecture Studio
Instituto Nazionale di Architettura, Rome, Italy 1988

Architecture Studio
Claude-Nicolas Ledoux Foundation, Arc and Senans, France 1988

Development techniques for a large project
Arcade Gallery, Carcassonne, France 1988

Architecture Studio, projects and constructions
School of Architecture, Lyons, France 1988

Architecture Studio
University of Pennsylvania, Philadelphia, United States 1988

Architecture Studio
Attems Palace, Vienna, Austria 1987

The city is an island: lighthouses in the city
Georges Pompidou Centre, Paris, France. Conference with Jean-Christophe Bailly. 1987

Architecture in building, research and leading-edge technology
French Institute of Architecture, Paris, France 1987

New habitats: the experience of residents with collective spaces
Higher School of Applied Art, Geneva, Switzerland 1987

Architecture Studio
Arc en Rêve, Bordeaux, France 1986

Berlin 84–Paris 89
International Centre for artistic experimentation, Boissano, Italy 1983

Building in old quarters
Boissano, Italy 1981

Presentation of the ACIH projects
Florence, Italy 1981

Teaching

School of Architecture, Montreal, Canada. April 1993, M. Robain & R. Tisnado.

University of Houston, Texas, United States. May 1993, A. Bretagnolle.

School of Architecture, Paris-La Défense, France. 1992/93, J.-F. Bonne.

Ecole supérieure d'architecture (ESA), France. 1991/92, M. Robain, R. Tisnado, J.-F. Bonne, A. Bretagnolle, R.-H. Arnaud.

University of Wisconsin, Milwaukee, United States. April 1990, R. Tisnado.

School of Architecture, Blacksburg, Virginia, United States. February 1989 R. Tisnado.

Bordeaux School of Architecture, France. 1983/1987, M. Robain.

Paris-Belleville School of Architecture (UP8), France. 1980/81, M. Robain.

Bibliography

Aizcorbe, Sanchez. "Trazo Maestro: Rodo Tisnado." *Caretas* (Argentina), (30 September 1991): p. 81.

À la recherche de l'urbanité. Exhibition catalogue of the first Paris Architecture Biennial Festival held at the Georges Pompidou Centre. Paris: Academy Editions, 1980.

Amsoneit, Wolfgang. *Contemporary European Architects.* Germany: Taschen, 1992, p. 32.

Architecture à prendre. Catalogue of national meetings on the architecture of teaching institutions, Béziers: Hérault Department Caue, 1991, pp. 44–45, 62–63.

"Architecture cinétique: 25 logements rue Domrémy à Paris." *Techniques & Architecture* (France) (No. 357, 1985): pp. 48–53.

Architecture contemporaine, 88/89. Switzerland: Anthony Krafft Editeur, 1988, pp. 210–215.

Architectures publiques. Brussels: Mardaga, 1990, pp. 21–22.

"Architecture Studio, las huellas de una plaza de Toros." *El Cronista* (Argentina) (18 March 1992).

"Architecture Studio." *Baumeister* (Germany) (No. 1, 1982).

Architecture Studio. Paris: Editions Techniques & Architecture, 1991.

Architecture Studio, in Arch. Exhibition catalogue. Rome: Carte Segrete, 1988.

Architecture Studio, Stimuli. Paris: Editions Champs Vallon and Les Editions du Demi-Cercle, 1987.

Architecture Studio. Exhibition catalogue. Bordeaux: Editions Arc-en-Rêve, 1986.

Architettura e spazio sacro nella modernità. Catalogue of the Venice Biennial Festival. Venice: Abitare Segesta Cataloghi, 1992, p. 225.

Arnaboldi, Mario Antonio. "Lycée des Arènes, Toulouse." *L'Arca* (Italy) (No. 69, 1993): pp. 30–37.

Arquitectura francesa, 11 proyectos, Sevilla. Exhibition catalogue. Seville: Junta de Andalucia, 1993, pp. 34–43, 64–71.

A travers l'architecture, 128 réalisations, 128 architectes. La Décade d'Architecture, Paris, 1983.

"Auf der Suche nach einer neuen Architektur im franzõsichen Wohnungsbau." *Stadt* (Germany) (August 1988): pp. 48–49.

"Bâtiment de la DDE, Poitiers." *Architecture d'aujourd'hui* (France) (No. 208, 1980).

"Bâtiment en continu—Collège Gasnier-Guy à Chelles." *Architecture d'aujourd'hui* (France) (No. 216, 1981): pp. 46–48.

Béhar, Michèle and Salama, Manuelle. *Paris Nouvelle/New Architecture.* Paris: Editions Techniques & Architecture, 1986.

Blin, Pascale. "Ambassade de France dans le sultanat d'Oman: du beau béton sous le soleil." *Le Moniteur* (France) (1 September 1989): pp. 58–62.

Bogar, Michal. "Lycée des Arènes, Toulouse." *Projekt* (Slovakia) (No. 2, 1992): pp. 116–117.

Boissière, Olivier. "Institut du Monde Arabe." *Architecture d'aujourd'hui* (France) (February 1988): pp. 1–22.

Boles, Daralice D. "Modernism in the City." *Progressive Architecture* (United States) (special issue, July1987): pp. 72–79, 86–87.

Borel, Yolande and Girard, Véronique. *Regards sur l'architecture.* Paris: Editions du Sorbier, 1990.

Borelli, Marina. "Architecture Studio, percorsi nel progetto." *Arredo Urbano* (Italy) (No. 47/48, 1993): pp. 74–79.

Brausch, Marianne. "Institut du Monde Arabe à Paris" *Le Moniteur* (France) (July 1989): pp. 30–31.

Brausch, Marianne. "Dunkerque, l'IUT croise la ville et l'océan." *Le Moniteur* (France) (No. 4530, 1990): pp. 122–125.

Cappiello, Vito. "Architecture Studio." *D'architettura* (Italy) (No. 9, 1993): pp. 54–65.

Catalogue du 3ème Salon International de l'Architecture. Paris: Editions Techniques & Architecture, 1990.

"Centre culturel Tihama à Djedda" *Archi Crée* (France) (No. 183, 1981).

Chirat, Sylvie. "Lycée Jules Verne, Cergy-le-Haut: Géométrie and polyvalence." *Construction Moderne* (France) (No. 77, 1994): pp 7–11.

Cohen, Jean-Louis and Lortie, André. *Des fortifs au périf.* Exhibition Catalogue of the exhibition held at the Arsenal Pavilion. Paris: Picard Editeur & Editions du Pavillon de l'Arsenal, 1992, p. 301.

Construire nel construito, conversazione en architettura moderna. Italy: Editions Kappa, 1989.

Cooper, Frederick. "Un coso reinventado." *Comerrio* (Peru) (28 April, 1993).

Davoine, Gilles."Amiens auscultée." *Le Moniteur* (France) (No. 4606, 1992) pp. 68–70.

"Découpage à Chelles, collège Gasnier-Guy" *Techniques & Architecture* (France) (No. 332, 1980).

"Des architectes pour réinventer la ville." *Murs-Murs* (France) (October 1988): pp. 26–27.

"Dix-neuf logements rue Domrémy, Paris 13e." *Architecture d'aujourd'hui* (France) (No. 253, 1987): pp. 2–3.

Doblado, Juan Carlo. "Arquitectura: creacion y sorpresa." *El Comerrio* (Peru) (August 1988).

"École maternelle et élémentaire rue Mouraud, Paris 20e." *Techniques & Architecture* (France) (No. 363, 1986).

Bibliography

Ellis, Charlotte. "Self-effacing IMA." *The Architectural Review* (Great Britain) (No. 1103, 1989): pp. 24–29.

"Erweitung des Krankenhauses von Montmorillon, Frankreich." *Architektur + Wettbewerbe* (Germany) (No. 117, 1984): pp. 30–31.

"Extension de l'hôpital de Montmorillon." *Architecture d'aujourd'hui* (France) (No. 227, 1983).

"Extension d'un service de médecine à Montmorillon. " *Techniques & Architecture* (France) (No. 324, 1980).

"Extension d'un service de médecine à Montmorillon." *Techniques & Architecture* (France) (No. 346, 1983).

Fuchigami, Yuki. "Architecture Studio, architect on the scene." *Kenchiku Bunka* (Japan) (No. 563, 1993): pp. 7–9.

Fuchigami, Yuki. "Logements rue du Château-des-Rentiers, Paris." *Tiling* (Japan) (No. 13, 1993): pp. 24–27.

Garcia Falco, Marta. "Architecture Studio: Modernos racionalistas franceses—technologia y contextualismo." *Clarin* (Argentina) (8 August 1994): pp. 4–5.

Garnier, Jacques. *Les lycées du futur*. Paris: L'Harmattan, 1991.

Gonzales Montaner, Humberto. "Un lugar para la imaginacion technologica." *Clarin* (Argentina) (30 January 1993): pp. 4–5.

Gonzales Montaner, Humberto. "Nuevos rumbos de la arquitectura francesa." *Clarin* (Argentina) (7 August 1992): pp. 4–7.

Goubert, Guillaume. "De nouveaux murs pour le parlement." *La Croix, l'événement* (France) (15 June 1994): p. 14.

Greco, Antonella. "C'è una casa pensante nel future." *La Repubblica Travaroma* (Italy) (23 April 1989).

Gromark, Sten. "Experiment i vardagen." Arkitektur (Sweden) (No. 7, 1988).

Gromark, Sten. *Paris Bygger*. Oslo: Svensk Byggt Jänsts, 1990.

Guennal, Dominique. "Liceo del futuro a Jaunay-Clan (Poitiers)." *Abacus* (Italy) (No. 15, 1988).

Gunsser, Christoph. "Gymnasium Jules Verne, Cergy—Geflügelter Ort." *Deutsche Bauzeitung* (Germany) (July 1994): p. 10.

"Gymnasium der Zukunft bei Poitiers." *Baumeister* (Germany) (No. 5, 1989): pp. 26–29.

"Habitation à Versailles." *Architecture d'aujourd'hui* (France) (No. 206, 1979).

"Héraud house—Montmorillon hospital" *A+U* (Japan) (No. 163, 1984): pp. 74–80.

"Hôpital de Montmorillon—Facade 9, boulevard Courcelles à Paris—École rue Mouraud à Paris—Logements rue Domrémy à Paris." *Space Design* (Japan) (No. 8502, 1985): pp. 27–29.

Houzelle, Béatrice. "L'informatique en pratique: École des Mines d'Albi-Carmaux et Centre de linguistique appliquée à Besancon." *Techniques & Architecture* (France) (No. 406, 1993): pp. 104–107.

Hoyet, Jean-Michel. "Architecture Studio, une technologie du signe." *Techniques & Architecture* (France) (No. 374, 1987).

Hoyet, Jean-Michel. *L'architecture contemporaine à Paris*. Paris: Editions Techniques & Architecture , 1994, pp. 51–83.

"I grattacieli puzzle." *Gente Viaggi* (Italy) (August 1988).

"Institut der Arabischen Welt." *Deutsche Bauzeitung* (Germany) (No. 19, 1985): pp. 46–47.

"Institut du Monde Arabe, Paris." *Deutsche Bauzeitung* (Germany) (No. 1645, 1988): p. 149.

"Institut du Monde Arabe." *Space Design* (Japan) (No. 05, 1987): pp. 42–45.

"Institut du Monde Arabe à Paris." *Architecture d'aujourd'hui* (France) (No. 231, 1984): pp. 23–29.

Institut du Monde Arabe à Paris. Etat d'architecture collection. Paris: Editions Champs Vallon, 1988.

Iritecna per l'Europa 1991. Italy: L'Arca Edizioni, 1991: pp. 80–81.

Jahn, Harald A. *Le nouveau Paris*. Iconothèque collection. Paris: Jean-Claude Lattès Editions, 1991, pp. 110—123.

Landes, Serge. "Notre-Dame de l'Arche d'Alliance." *Communio* (France) (Vol. 15, 1990): pp. 71–86.

Laporte, Raffaële. "Chroniques domotiques: Centre de vie pour étudiants à Jaunay-Clan." *L'Homme et l'Architecture* (France) (No. 10, 1991): pp. 26–27.

Lebrun, Jean. "Une église-phare pour Paris." *La Croix, l'événement* (France) (29 April 1987).

Catalogue of the exhibition held at the Arsenal Pavilion. *Le fer à Paris*. Paris: Editions Picard, 1989.

Le Futuroscope. Paris: Editions du Moniteur, 1992.

Lenglart, Denis and Vince, Agnès. *Universités, écoles supérieures*. Paris: Editions du Moniteur, 1992, p. 117.

Lenne, Frédéric. "Un centre de vie pour étudiants branchés." *Le Moniteur* (France) (No. 4518, 1990): pp. 147–148.

"Le 'pietre miliari' della città gli 'Stimoli' di Architecture Studio." *Metamorfosi* (Italy) (January/February 1988): pp. 14–15, 25–31.

Lesnikowski, Wojciech. "Arènes technical school, Toulouse." *Progressive Architecture* (United States) (April 1991): pp. 110–111.

Lesnikowski, Wojciech. *The new French Architecture*. New York: Rizzoli International Publications, 1990.

"L'espace partagé, ensemble de logements à Poitiers." *Techniques & Architecture* (France) (No. 335, 1980).

"L'Institut du Monde Arabe a Parigi." *L'Arca* (Italy) (No. 6, 1987): pp. 28–35.

"Loft pour quatre—agence Architecture Studio." *Archi Crée* (France) (No. 179, 1980).

"Logements rue Domrémy à Paris." *Archi Crée* (France) (No. 192, 1983).

"Logements rue Domrémy à Paris." *Techniques & Architecture* (France) (No. 343, 1982).

"Logements rue du Château-des-Rentiers, Paris." *Office Age* (Japan) (April 1988) pp. 24–25.

"Logements SAP à Poitiers—essai d'urbanisme atomique." *Architecture d'aujourd'hui* (France) (No. 211, 1980).

"Logements SAP à Poitiers, une échelle d'échange." *Techniques & Architecture* (France) (No. 312, 1979).

Loriers, Marie-Christine. "Lycée des Arènes à Toulouse." *Techniques & Architecture* (France) (No. 400, 1992): pp. 122–129.

Loriers, Marie-Christine. "Université de la Citadelle à Dunkerque." *Techniques & Architecture* (France) (No. 393, 1991): pp. 15–19.

Loriers, Marie-Christine. "Concours pour la Fédération francaise de judo." *Techniques & Architecture* (France) (No. 383, 1989): pp. 28–29.

Loriers, Marie-Christine. "Architecture Studio, une pointe de métal." *Beaux-Arts* (France) (No. 57, 1988): pp. 79–82.

Loriers, Marie-Christine. "Through the looking glass." *Progressive Architecture* (United States) (May 1988): pp. 94–98.

"Lycée du Futur, Jaunay-Clan." *Arkitekt Företaget* (Sweden) (No. 5, 1989): pp. 6–7.

"Maison de convalescence à Clamart." *Archi Crée* (France) (No. 175, 1980).

"Maison de convalescence à Clamart & Hôpital de Montmorillon." *Techniques & Architecture* (France) (No. 324 , 1979): pp. 69–71.

"Maison Héraud à Chasseneuil du Poitou: une folie contemporaine." *La Maison de Marie-Claire* (France) (No. 194, 1983): pp. 99–103.

Mandrelli, Doriana O. "Il polo universitario di Dunkerque." *L'Arca* (Italy) (No. 48, 1991): pp. 22–33.

Mandrelli, Doriana O. "Architecture Studio." *Controspazio* (Italy) (March/April 1990): pp. 10–13.

Marchisio, Jean-Claude. "Strasbourg, le chantier de l'Europe." *Les Dernières Nouvelles d'Alsace* (France) (5 October 1992).

Martin, Hervé. *Guide de l'architecture moderne à Paris.* Paris: Edition Syros-Alternative, 1991, pp. 36, 97, 136, 137, 153, 173.

"Martin Robain." *Daidelos* (Germany) (No. 40, 1991): pp. 72–73.

Matthews, Thomas. "A discourse of symbols: the recent work of Architecture Studio." *Architectural Record* (Great Britain) (January 1987).

Mazenod (de), Sophie. "Poste de commandement, caserne des sapeurs-pompiers, Gennevilliers: Une minute pour l'architecte." *Topos* (France) (No. 10, 1992): pp. 68–69.

Morin, Francoise. "Le roman de l'IMA." *Dynasteurs* (France) (December 1987): pp. 82–86.

Ortiz de Zevallos, Augusto. "De como edificar metaforas." *Debate* (Spain) (May/June 1988): p. 59.

Pagliari, Francesco. "Il parlamento europeo a Strasburgo." *L'Arca* (Italy) (No. 60, 1992): pp. 32–39.

Paris, Architecture et utopie, projets architecturaux pour l'entrée dans le 21e siècle. Arsenal Pavilion exhibition catalogue. Berlin: Kristin Feireiss Publishers, 1988.

Paris, la ville et ses projets. Paris: Editions Babylone & Editions du Pavillon de l'Arsenal, 1992, pp. 55, 61, 220, 259, 266.

Paris Moderne 1977–1986. Paris: Editions l'Equerre, 1986.

Pedinielli, Michèle. "Architecture Studio, un projet pour l'Europe." *L'Etudiant* (France) (November 1991): pp. 78–79.

Pelissier, Alain. "Institut du monde arabe à Paris: Transmoderne." *Techniques & Architecture* (France) (No. 376, 1988): pp. 124–137.

Pelissier, Alain. "Institut du monde arabe à Paris, la technologie mise en signes." *Techniques & Architecture* (France) (No. 350, 1983): pp. 139–154.

Péroncel-Hugoz, Jean-Pierre. "Une maison de France sur le Golfe Persique." *Le Monde* (France) (2 March 1991).

Peters, Paulhans. *Paris, die grossen Projekte.* Germany: Ernst & Sohn, 1992, pp. 62–73.

Picard, Denis . "Des formes pour l'information—Lycée du futur à Jaunay-Clan." *Connaissance des Arts* (France) (February 1990): pp. 108–112.

Pisani, Mario. "Liceo Jules Verne a Cergy-le-Haut, progetto di Architecture Studio." *Controspazio* (Italy) (No. 3, 1994): pp. 30–37.

Pisani, Mario. "Dialogo con Rodo Tisnado di Architecture Studio." *Costruire in Laterizio* (Italy) (No. 41, 1994): pp. 428–431.

Pisani, Mario. "L'Ambasciata di Francia nel Sultanato dell'Oman." *L'industria delle Costruzioni* (Italy) (No. 269, 1994): pp. 16–19.

Pisani, Mario. "Architecture Studio: progetti e opere recenti." *L'industria delle Costruzioni* (Italy) (No. 249/50, 1992) pp. 4–25.

Pisani, Mario. "Institut du Monde Arabe, Paris—Body building." *Art Forum International* (United States) (April 1988): pp. 101–107.

Bibliography

Pisani, Mario. "Incontri Rodo Tisnado—Architecture Studio." *Casa Vogue* (Italy) (February 1988): pp. 130–131.

Pisani, Mario. *Tendenze nell'architettura degli anni '90.* Italy: Edizioni Dedalo, 1989.

Pousse, Jean-Francois. "Parlement Européen à Strasbourg." *Techniques & Architecture* (France) (No. 400, 1992): pp. 46–47.

Pousse, Jean-Francois. "Un patio dans le désert. Ambassade de France, Mascate, Oman." *Techniques & Architecture* (France) (No. 388, 1990): pp. 74–79.

"Projet pour les archives régionales du Monde du Travail à Roubaix." *Techniques & Architecture* (France) (No. 362, 1985).

Proust, Guilène. "L'École des Mines d'Albi, un lieu pour les génies de l'innovation." *Art Volume* (France) (No. 7, 1994): p. 34.

Quai Branly. French Institute of Architecture exhibition catalogue. Rome: Carte Segrete, 1990, pp. 186–189.

Rambert, Francis. "Archi Sacré." *D'Architectures* (France) (No. 45, 1994): pp. 22–26.

Redecke, Sebastian. "Europäisches Parlament in Strassburg." *Bauwelt* (Germany) (No. 23, 1994): p. 1240.

Righetti, Paolo. "La chiesa dedicata Notre-Dame de l'Arche d'Alliance." *L'Arca* (Italy) (No. 74, 1993): pp. 66–71.

Robichon, Francois. "Construire l'Europe." *D'Architectures* (France) (No. 32, 1993): pp. 38–42.

Roca, Miguel Angel. "Es necesario estar atentu, equipo Architecture Studio." *Notas desde el Sur* (Argentina) (No. 1, 1993): pp. 42–48.

Roodbol, Jos. "IMA." *De Architect* (Sweden) (No. 19, 1988).

Salon, Didier. "Des arènes au lycée." *Construction Moderne* (France) (No. 73, 1992): pp. 28–33.

Schamberger, Jean-Charles ."Lycée du Futuroscope, le jeu subtil de la transparence." *Néo Restauration* (France) (No. 231, 1991): pp. 42–43.

Séville 1992. Exhibition catalogue. Rome: Carte Segrete, 1992: pp. 134–139.

Sprang, Philippe. "Tête de la Défense, ce projet qui remet la dalle en question." *Le Figaro* (France) (5 February 1990).

Stocchi, Attilio. "Ultimi designi a Parigi: Architecture Studio." *Costruire* (Italy) (No. 115, 1992): pp. 59–60.

"Une base de vie à Poitiers: cité universitaire à Jaunay-Clan." *Archi Crée* (France) (No. 240, 1991): pp. 90–93.

Welsh, John. "Restoring its spirit." *Building Design* (Great Britain) (No. 1073, 1992): p. 16.

Welsh, John. "Architecture Studio." *Building Design* (Great Britain) (No. 1064, 1992): p. 16.

Wissenbach, Vincente. "Architecture Studio: Arquitectura coletiva em busca da mutacao." *Projeto* (Brazil) (No. 163, 1993): pp. 45–49.

Wissenbach, Vincente. "Architecture Studio, a technologia apenas como um meio e nao como um fim em si mesma." *Projeto* (Brazil) (No. 124, 1989): pp. 88–89.

Wustlich, Reinhart. Centrum-Jahrbuch *Architektur und Stadt*, 1993. Germany: Vieweg, 1993: pp. 241–247.

Acknowledgments

Credits for the selected and current projects

A number on its own corresponds to the page on which the photographer's work is featured. Commonly, all pictures on the page belong to the same photographer, however, where several artists are featured on the same page, the corresponding image is listed in brackets by its caption number.

Photos and illustrations

Abbadie (Hervé): 97; 98; 99; 119; 121; 122; 123; 124; 125.

Anicki & Achdou: 128 (5,7).

Antraygues (Michel): 135 (3).

Barral Baron (Marc): 103; 104; 105 (9).

Bechet (Michel): 154; 155; 156; 157; 158; 159; 160; 161.

Couturier (Stéphane): 70 (14); 81; 82; 83; 86; 88; 89; 105 (7); 108 (13); 109; 127; 128(6); 129; 135(4); 141; 142; 143; 169 (4); 170 (8); 171; 172; 173 (13,15); 174; 175 (19); 178; 179; 180; 181; 185; 186; 187; 192; 193; 194; 196; 197; 198; 199; 200; 201; 210; 211.

Denancé (Michel): 25; 26.

Gaston: 46 (5); 52 (3); 53 (5); 72; 73; 77; 79; 85; 91(5); 92; 95; 102; 111; 112; 113; 114; 115; 117; 120; 130; 131; 133; 136; 163; 164; 166; 170 (7); 175 (18); 177 (3); 182; 189; 190; 191; 209 (3); 217 (1); 221 (10); 230 (34); 231 (37); 232 (41).

Gouillardon (Alain): 169 (6).

Guérin (Gilles): 67; 69.

Moch (Michel): 105 (8); 106; 107; 108 (12).

Monfaucon (Christophe, de): 29; 54; 55; 56; 57; 58; 59; 60; 61.

Rosais: 183.

Seigneur (François): 100-101; 229 (31); 244 (77).

Sieff (Jean-Loup): 8.

Saint-Chamas (Thibaut, de): 9; 10; 11; 13; 208; 209 (2); 214.

Tossan (Olivier): 76.

Tourneboeuf (Patrick): 137; 138; 139; 145; 146; 147; 148; 149; 150; 151; 152; 153.

Urquijo (Fernando) et Rhiel (Michel): 39; 40; 41; 62; 63; 64; 65; 66; 68; 70 (15); 71.

Index

Bold page numbers refer to projects
included in Selected and Current Works

Every effort has been made to trace the original source of copyright material contained in this book. The publishers would be pleased to hear from copyright holders to rectify any errors or omissions.

The information and illustrations in this publication have been prepared and supplied by Architecture Studio. While all reasonable efforts have been made to ensure accuracy, the publishers do not, under any circumstance, accept responsibility for errors, omissions and representations express or implied.

The translation of this manuscript has been completed and proofed by highly qualified and accredited translators. While every effort has been taken to ensure its accuracy and correctness, no responsibility, financial or otherwise will be accepted by The Images Publishing Group for any errors or omissions.